THE AUTUMN FRUITS COOKBOOK

BY

CHARLOTTE POPESCU

CAVALIER COOKBOOKS

An imprint of Cavalier Paperbacks

Published by Cavalier Cookbooks 1999
Reprinted 2002
Reprinted 2008

An imprint of Cavalier Paperbacks
Burnham House,
Upavon,
Wilts SN9 6DU

Cover illustration by Beverley Lees

ISBN 978-1-899470-52-5

Printed and bound in Great Britain by CPI Cox & Wyman, Cardiff Road, Reading, Berks

CONTENTS

NOTES FOR THE COOK

If you have a fan-assisted electric oven reduce the specified heat in the recipes by 10 - 20°C.

1 teaspoon = 5 ml
1 tablespoon = 15ml

SHORTCRUST PASTRY

Shortcrust pastry is required in a number of recipes. To make the pastry use the required amount of flour and margarine. Usually the margarine is half the amount of flour. Rub the margarine into the flour with your fingertips. Use a little cold water to bind the mixture together and roll out as specified in the recipe.

PEARS

STARTERS

PEA, PEAR AND MINT SOUP

This soup can be served hot or cold. If you decide to serve it cold, swirl a dollop of crème fraîche into each bowl of soup before serving.

Serves 8

3 tbsp sunflower oil
2 onions, skinned and chopped
450g, 1lb peas, defrosted if frozen
3 pears, peeled, cored and chopped
1.2l, 2pt chicken stock
salt and pepper
juice of ½ lemon
a handful of apple mint (just the leaves)

Cook the chopped onions in the oil in a saucepan for 5 minutes. Then add the peas, chopped pears and the chicken stock. Half-cover the pan with a lid and simmer for 20 minutes. Process or liquidize the soup and season with salt, pepper and lemon juice. Lastly, chop the mint leaves and stir them into the soup.

PEARS IN CREAM DRESSING

Serves 4

1 egg
juice of ½ lemon
1 tbsp light brown sugar
4 tbsp double cream
1 tsp tarragon
2 large pears, peeled, halved and cored
few sprigs of watercress
50g, 2oz (½ cup) walnuts, chopped

Beat the egg with the lemon juice and sugar in a bowl. Then place the bowl over a pan of simmering water. Stir until the mixture thickens and then set aside to cool. Whip the cream and fold in the egg mixture and the tarragon. Pour the cream dressing over the top of each halved pear. Decorate with watercress and chopped walnuts.

STILTON PEARS

Stilton and pears go wonderfully well together.

Serves 4

2 large pears
2 tbsp lemon juice
50g, 2oz curd cheese
75g, 3oz Stilton cheese, crumbled
2 tbsp sunflower oil
1 tbsp mayonnaise
pinch of mustard powder
pinch of sugar
1 tsp poppy seeds
salt and pepper

Use an apple corer to core the pears and make a cavity. Sprinkle some lemon juice into each hole. Cream together the two cheeses and press as much of this mixture into the cavities of the pears as you can. Chill the pears while you make the dressing. Whisk the oil, mayonnaise, remaining lemon juice, mustard, sugar, poppy seeds, salt and pepper together. Spoon the dressing onto four plates. Cut each pear in half and make slices of pears, fanning them out over the dressing on the plates. Serve at once.

PEARS WITH CAMEMBERT SAUCE

A very easy starter and one that's quick to prepare.

Serves 4

4 ripe pears, peeled, halved and cored
1 tbsp lemon juice
150ml, ¼pt (⅔ cup) soured cream
2 tbsp double cream
50g, 2oz Camembert cheese, chopped
pinch of cayenne pepper

Brush the pears with lemon juice. Put the soured cream, double cream and Camembert into a food processor and blend until smooth. Pour the sauce over the halved pears and sprinkle with cayenne pepper.

GOAT'S CHEESE WITH PEAR AND
WALNUT SALAD

This makes an excellent starter for a dinner party.

Serves 4

A few lettuce leaves
100g, 4oz goat's cheese, halved into two circles
2 ripe pears, cored and cut into chunks
50g, 2oz (½ cup) walnuts
handful of chopped watercress
1 tbsp lemon juice
2 tbsp oil

Arrange the goat's cheese on the lettuce leaves. Mix together the pears, walnuts and watercress. Combine the lemon juice and oil and pour over the salad ingredients. Serve on top of the circles of goat's cheese.

PEAR AND HAM STARTER

Serves 8

450g, 1lb firm pears, peeled, cored and chopped
450g, 1lb leeks, chopped
4 cloves of garlic, peeled
75g, 3oz (⅓ cup) butter
1 tsp caster sugar
8 slices of smoked ham
lettuce leaves

Dressing

4 tbsp olive oil
2 tbsp white wine vinegar
1 tsp mustard powder
salt and pepper
sprinkling of dried mixed herbs

Place the leeks with the pears and garlic in a saucepan of boiling water. Reduce to a simmer and cook gently for 15 minutes. Drain and put in a food processor with the butter and caster sugar and blend to a purée. Meanwhile lay out the slices of ham and when the purée is cold lay some on each piece of ham. Roll up the slices and arrange on lettuce leaves on a plate. Combine the oil, vinegar, mustard, herbs and seasoning and spoon a little dressing over each ham roll. Serve at once.

PEARS VINAIGRETTE

Serves 8

4 ripe pears, peeled, cored, and sliced

Dressing

4 tbsp sunflower oil
juice of 1 lemon
salt and pepper
1 tsp caster sugar
1 tsp chopped mint
1 tsp chopped parsley

Arrange the sliced pears on a serving plate. Make the dressing by combining the oil, lemon juice, sugar, salt and pepper. Add the parsley and mint and pour immediately over the halved pears.

PEARS WITH CHEESE AND APPLES

Serves 4

100g, 4oz Cheddar cheese, grated
1 red-skinned eating apple, Spartan or Royal Gala,
cored and chopped
25g, 1oz (¼ cup) walnuts
25g, 1oz (¼ cup) raisins
4 tbsp milk
Worcestershire sauce
2 pears, halved and cored
lemon juice

Put the cheese, apple, walnuts, raisins and milk in a bowl
and mix well. Season with a few drops of Worcestershire
sauce. Sprinkle the halved pears with a little lemon juice
and pile the cheese and apple mixture on the top of each
pear half.

PEAR AND TUNA SALAD

A good, nutritious salad which can be served for a light
lunch with warm crusty brown bread.

Serves 6

4 pears, Williams preferably, peeled, cored and diced
450g, 1lb flaked tuna
bunch of lettuce leaves
juice of 2 lemons
4 tbsp olive oil
1 tbsp chopped parsley
2 tsp chopped chives

Mix the tuna with the diced pears and arrange over a bed
of lettuce. Sprinkle with the lemon juice and the oil and
scatter the herbs over the tuna and pears.

PEAR, MELON AND CUCUMBER SALAD

Serves 8

4 pears
1 melon
1 cucumber

Dressing

5 tbsp olive oil
3 tbsp lemon juice
1 tbsp sugar
1 tsp salt
sprinkling of pepper
2 tsp French mustard

Peel and cut the fruit and cucumber into chunks. Mix together the oil, lemon juice, sugar, salt, pepper and mustard and marinade the fruits in the dressing for at least an hour before serving.

PEAR AND AVOCADO SALAD

Serves 4

2 pears, Williams preferably, peeled, cored and sliced
1 avocado, peeled and sliced
juice of 1 lemon
handful of chopped lettuce
225g, 8oz Wensleydale cheese
4 tbsp olive oil
1 tbsp white wine vinegar
salt and pepper
8 slices of Parma ham

Put the pear and avocado slices in a bowl and sprinkle with lemon juice. Cut the cheese into small pieces and mix with the lettuce. Make the dressing by combining the oil, vinegar and some salt and pepper. Spread out the pieces of Parma ham and arrange the pear and avocado slices and cheese and lettuce over the ham. Pour the vinaigrette over the top and serve at once.

PEAR AND CHEESE FLAN

This combination of pears and cheese makes an interesting flan which makes a change from the more usual bacon quiche.

Serves 6

Pastry

75g, 3oz (¾ cup) plain flour
75g, 3oz (¾ cup) wholemeal plain flour
75g, 3oz (⅓ cup) butter
2 tbsp water

Filling

4 tbsp milk
2 tbsp single cream
100g, 4oz Stilton cheese, crumbled
2 eggs, beaten
2 ripe Conference pears, peeled, cored and sliced

Make the pastry by adding the butter to the two flours and rubbing with your fingertips until the mixture resembles breadcrumbs. Add the water and bind together. Use to line a 20cm (8in) greased flan tin. Cook blind in the oven at gas mark 5, 190°C (375°F) for 10 minutes. Mix together the milk, cream, cheese and eggs. Arrange the pears on the base of the cooked flan case and pour the cheese mixture over the pears. Bake for about 20 minutes until set.

HERRINGS ROLLED IN PEARS AND OATS

Serves 4

2 herrings, cleaned with tails intact but heads removed
225g, 8oz pears, peeled, cored and chopped
50g, 2oz onion, peeled and diced
50g, 2oz (½ cup) coarse oatmeal
grated rind of 1 small lime
50g, 2oz (¼ cup) butter

Cut each fish in half lengthways. Coat the pears in oatmeal. Fry the onion, and grated lime rind with the pears in half the butter. Place a little stuffing on each herring fillet. Roll up and secure with cocktail sticks. Place in a greased ovenproof dish and dot with remaining butter. Bake at gas mark 5, 190°C (375°F) for 30 minutes.

RED CABBAGE BAKED WITH PEARS

This vegetable side dish would go well with gammon or pork.

Serves 6 - 8

1 garlic clove, peeled and crushed
900g, 2lb red cabbage, finely shredded
2 large pears, peeled, cored and sliced
salt and pepper
150ml, ¼pt (⅔ cup) chicken stock
2 tbsp lemon juice

Rub the garlic round the sides of a casserole. Spoon half the cabbage into the dish, followed by a layer of pear slices. Season with salt and pepper. Repeat the layers. Pour over the stock and lemon juice. Cover and bake at gas mark 3, 160°C (325°F) for about 2 hours.

MAIN DISHES

CHICKEN AND PEAR CASSEROLE

Serves 4 - 6

4 chicken pieces
2 tbsp sunflower oil
1 onion, peeled and sliced
1 small can of prunes
450g, 1lb Conference pears, peeled, cored and quartered
2 tbsp flour
1 chicken stock cube
150ml, ¼pt (⅔ cup) dry white wine
grated rind of 1 lemon
salt and pepper

Heat the oil in a large frying pan and brown the chicken pieces. Place in a casserole. Fry the onion in the same pan for 5 minutes and add to the chicken. Drain the prunes, reserve the syrup from the can and make it up to 150ml, ¼pt (⅔ cup) with water. Spoon the prunes and pears over the chicken. Stir the flour into the pan juices and cook for a minute. Add the stock cube, prune syrup and wine. Bring to the boil and stir, cooking for a minute or two. Add the lemon rind, salt and pepper and pour over the chicken. Cook in the oven at gas mark 5, 190°C (375°F) for 1 hour.

SPICY LAMB WITH PEARS

Serves 4 - 6

900g, 2lb cubed lamb
2 onions, peeled and chopped
2 tbsp olive oil
¼ tsp coriander
¼ tsp ginger
¼ tsp cinnamon
225g 8oz dried pears, soaked in water and drained
2 tbsp honey
300ml, ½pt (1¼ cups) chicken stock
salt and pepper
1 tbsp cornflour, blended to a paste with a little water

Put the lamb, onions, olive oil, spices, pears, honey and stock into a casserole. Season, cover and cook in the oven at gas mark 3, 160°C (325°F) for 2 hours. Arrange the lamb and pears in a serving dish. Pour the sauce into a small saucepan and stir in the cornflour paste. Bring to the boil and stir until thickened. Pour the sauce over the lamb and serve.

LAMB BAKED WITH WINE, PEARS AND HONEY

Serves 6

1 small shoulder or leg of lamb
1 tbsp flour
1 tsp ground bay leaves
1 clove of garlic, peeled
90ml, 3fl oz (⅓ cup) red wine
2 tbsp honey
4 pears, peeled, cored and quartered
2 tsp cornflour, blended to a paste with a little water

Mix the ground bay leaves with the flour. Rub the lamb all over with the clove of garlic and the flour. Place the meat in a roasting tin with the wine and bake at gas mark 4, 180°C (350°F), allowing 25 minutes for every 450g, 1lb of meat. Turn the joint and baste it after an hour. When the cooking time is over, lift the meat out and drain, reserving the liquid. Return the meat to the tin and spread the honey over the meat. Add the pears and cook in the oven for a further 30 minutes. Serve the meat surrounded by the pears. Remove as much fat as possible from the reserved liquid and make a sauce by adding a little water and the cornflour paste. Heat and serve the sauce separately.

PORK AND PEARS

Serves 4

4 pork chops
25g, 1oz (2 tbsp) butter
2 large pears, preferably Conference, cored and halved
1 tbsp marjoram
1 tbsp lemon juice
salt and pepper

Melt the butter in a large frying pan and add the chops. Brown the chops on both sides. Place in a single layer in a greased ovenproof dish. Sprinkle with salt and pepper. Lightly poach the pears in a little water until soft. Drain, reserving the juice. Place a pear half on each chop. Heat the reserved juice in a pan with the marjoram and lemon juice. Bring to the boil, and boil rapidly until reduced by half. Pour over the chops, then cover the dish. Bake in the oven at gas mark 4, 180°C (350°F) for 40 minutes.

ORCHARD PORK

Serve this pork dish with mashed potato and broccoli.

Serves 6

450g, 1lb pears, peeled, cored and sliced
3 eating apples, preferably Cox's, peeled,
cored and sliced
lemon juice
900g, 2lb spare-rib pork chops
25g, 1oz (2 tbsp) butter
2 tbsp olive oil
1 onion, peeled and sliced
2 tbsp reducrrant jelly
450ml, ¾pt (1½ cups) chicken stock
300ml, ½pt (1¼ cups) cider
1 bay leaf

Toss the apple and pear slices in lemon juice. Cut the pork into smallish pieces. Heat the butter and olive oil in a casserole and fry the pork for 5 minutes until browned. Remove and fry the onion. Return the pork and add the redcurrant jelly, chicken stock, cider and bay leaf. Bring to the boil, cover and simmer for 45 minutes. Add the apples and pears and cook for another 30 minutes. Strain off the liquid and boil it rapidly in a separate saucepan until reduced by half. Pour back over the meat and serve.

BACON CHOPS WITH PEARS

A simple but very tasty way of serving bacon chops.

Serves 6

6 bacon chops
3 pears, peeled, cored and sliced
25g, 1oz (2 tbsp) butter, melted
2 tbsp flour
1 egg, beaten
3 tbsp breadcrumbs
oil

Brush the bacon chops with the melted butter and grill for 5 minutes on each side. Coat the pear slices with flour, and then with egg and breadcrumbs. Fry in the oil for 10 minutes until golden brown. Serve the bacon with a couple of pear slices on the top of each one.

PUDDINGS

PEARS IN FUDGE SAUCE

6 pears, peeled, cored and quartered
300ml, ½pt (1¼ cups) water
50g, 2oz (⅓ cup) sugar

Fudge sauce

150g, 6oz (1½ cups) light brown sugar
25g, 1oz (2 tbsp) butter
2 tbsp water
150ml, ¼pt (⅔ cup) single cream
150ml, ¼pt double cream, whipped

First dissolve the sugar in the water by cooking over a gentle heat. Poach the pear quarters in this syrup. As soon as the pears are tender remove them from the syrup and cool. Slice the pears into a serving bowl. To make the sauce, put the sugar, butter and water in a saucepan and heat gently to dissolve the sugar. Boil until the mixture forms a ball when a little is dropped into cold water. Take off the heat and stir in the single cream. Allow to cool and then stir into the whipped double cream. Pour over the pears and chill.

BAKED PEARS

If you have a sweet tooth and love condensed milk, this is the dish for you.

2 large pears, peeled, cored and halved
2 tbsp pine nuts
1 tsp ground nutmeg
150ml, ¼pt (⅔ cup) condensed milk
4 tbsp Marsala
50g, 2oz (⅓ cup) demerara sugar
crème fraîche, to serve

Mix the pine nuts with the nutmeg and press into the hollows in the pears. Arrange the pears, hollowed-out side down, in a shallow ovenproof dish. Mix the condensed milk with the sherry and pour over the pears. Cover and bake for 40 minutes or until the pears are tender. Leave to cool. Sprinkle the sugar over the pears and grill for a few minutes until caramelised. Leave to cool. Serve chilled with crème fraîche.

POACHED RED PEARS

This makes an easy and deliciously light dinner party dessert.

4 large pears, peeled but with stalks left on
50g, 2oz (⅓ cup) caster sugar
300ml, ½pt (1¼ cups) red wine
2 cloves

Put the sugar, wine and cloves into a saucepan and heat gently until sugar has dissolved. Add pears, standing them upright, and cover, simmering gently for 15 minutes. Baste every so often with the liquid. Remove the pears and return pan to a high heat. Boil until the liquid has reduced by half. Pour the liquid over the pears and serve hot or cold.

CHOCOLATE COVERED PEARS

Pears and chocolate make an excellent combination. This pudding is quick and easy to prepare.

100g, 4oz plain chocolate
4 tbsp rum
15g, ½oz (1 tbsp) butter
4 pears, peeled and cored
50g, 2oz (½ cup) hazelnuts, chopped

Melt the chocolate, rum and butter in a bowl over a saucepan of boiling water. Stir until smooth. Pour over the pears and sprinkle with the chopped hazelnuts.

CARAMELISED PEARS WITH BRANDY

6 pears, peeled
juice and rind of 1 small lemon
1 tsp ground cinnamon
150g, 6oz (1 cup) granulated sugar
2 tbsp brandy
1 tbsp cornflour blended to a smooth paste with a little
water

Sprinkle the lemon juice over the peeled pears and put in a saucepan. Pour in a little water. Add the grated lemon rind and cinnamon. Cover and bring to the boil. Then reduce the heat and simmer for 20 minutes. Meanwhile, put the sugar in a heavy based saucepan and heat to a light golden colour. Remove from the heat and cool. Pour the liquid that the pears have been cooking in, onto the caramel and stir to dissolve it over a gentle heat. Put the pears in the caramel liquid and add the brandy. Cover and cook gently for a further 10 minutes. Remove the pears and put in a serving bowl. Mix the cornflour with the water and add to the caramel liquid. Bring to the boil, and then simmer for a couple of minutes stirring all the time. Pour over the pears and serve at once.

PEAR AND KIWI FRUIT CRUNCH

This makes a delicious, nutritious, fruity pudding, loved by adults and children alike.

3 ripe pears, peeled, cored and sliced
juice of ½ lemon
3 kiwi fruit, peeled and sliced
50g, 2oz (¼ cup) butter
100g, 4oz (1 cup) brown breadcrumbs
50g, 2oz (½ cup) brown sugar
small tub of crème fraîche

Layer the pears at the bottom of a serving bowl, sprinkle with lemon juice and cover with the sliced kiwi fruit. Melt the butter in the frying pan and fry the breadcrumbs with the sugar until crisp. Spread over the fruit. Cover with a layer of crème fraîche.

PEARS IN CREAM

This is a quick, easy pudding.

4 pears, peeled, cored and sliced
50g, 2oz (¼ cup) butter
150ml, ¼pt (⅔ cup) double cream
25g, 1oz (¼ cup) light soft brown sugar

Heat the butter in a frying pan and fry the slices of pear gently for a few minutes until tender. Turn into an ovenproof dish. Pour over the cream and bake in the oven at gas mark 4, 180°C (350°F) for about 15 minutes. Remove from the oven and sprinkle with the brown sugar before serving.

PEAR AND CRANBERRY TRIFLE

10 sponge fingers
240ml, 8fl oz (1 cup) sweet white wine

6 pears, peeled, cored and sliced
225g, 8oz (1 ⅓ cups) sugar
450g, 1lb cranberries

Topping

2 eggs, separated
50g, 2oz (⅓ cup) caster sugar
225g, 8oz (2 cups) mascarpone
1 tbsp brandy

Layer the sponge fingers on the bottom of a serving bowl. Pour the wine over them. Poach the pears in a syrup of 4 tablespoons of water and 100g, 4oz (⅔ cup) of the sugar for 15 minutes. Cook the cranberries for 10 minutes in the remaining sugar. Lay the pears on the sponge finger base and cover with the cranberries. Whisk the egg yolks with the sugar until thick and creamy. Gradually beat in the mascarpone and brandy. Lastly fold in the stiffly beaten egg whites. Top the trifle with this mixture and chill.

PEAR AND MACAROON PIE

Pastry

225g, 8oz (2 cups) self-raising flour
150g, 6oz (¾ cup) butter
4 tbsp milk

Filling

125g, 5oz (¾ cup) granulated sugar
425ml, 14fl oz (1½ cups) water
900g, 2lb pears, peeled, quartered and cored
50g, 2oz macaroons
3 tbsp Marsala
60ml, 2fl oz (¼ cup) double cream
15g, ½oz (½ tbsp) caster sugar

Rub the butter into the flour and bind together with a little
of the milk to make the pastry. Wrap the dough in cling
film and chill. Dissolve the sugar in the water by heating it
gently. Add the pears to the syrup and cook until just tender. Remove the pears and leave to cool. Pour the Marsala
over the macaroons and allow to soak in. Cut the pastry in
half and roll out two circles. Use one to line the base of a
greased 23cm (9in) pie plate. Cover the pastry with the
pears and then arrange the soaked macaroons on top. Pour
over the cream. Cover with the remaining circle of pastry.
Brush the top with some of the milk and sprinkle on the
caster sugar. Bake in the oven at gas mark 6, 200°C (400°F)
for about 40 minutes.

PEAR AND ALMOND PIE

*shortcrust pastry made with 225g, 8oz (2 cups) plain
flour and 100g, 4oz (½ cup) margarine*

*225g, 8oz (2 cups) ground almonds
50g, 2oz (⅓ cup) caster sugar
4 tbsp sherry
4 pears, peeled, cored and sliced
juice of ½ lemon*

Roll out two thirds of the pastry and line a greased 20cm
(8in) pie dish. Stir the almonds with the sugar and sherry
to make a crumbly mixture. Spread this mixture over the
pastry base. Toss the pear slices in the lemon juice and
drain off any excess. Arrange the pear slices over the almond mixture. Roll out the remaining pastry and place over
the pears. Dampen the edges of the pastry base with milk
or water and cover with the lid and press the edges down
to seal in the filling. Make a small hole to allow steam to
escape. Brush with milk and sprinkle with a little caster
sugar, if liked. Bake in the oven at gas mark 4, 180°C
(350°F) for 40 minutes.

PEAR TARTE TATIN

This makes a change from the more usual apple tarte tatin.

Pastry

150g, 6oz (1½ cup) plain flour
75g, 3oz (⅓ cup) butter
2 tbsp icing sugar
1 egg yolk
1 tbsp water

25g, 1oz (2 tbsp) butter
50g, 2oz (⅓ cup) caster sugar
4 pears, peeled, cored and sliced
cream, to serve

To make the pastry, process all the ingredients or rub the butter into the flour and icing sugar. Bind together with the egg yolk and water and knead lightly. Chill for 30 minutes before rolling out. Meanwhile, melt the butter and sugar together over a gentle heat and then spread over the bottom of a 20cm (8in) flan tin. Arrange the pears over the butter and sugar. Roll the pastry into a circle and fit over the pears, sealing down well at the sides. Bake in the oven at gas mark 4, 180°C (350°F) for 30 minutes. The pastry should be golden brown. Remove from the oven and invert onto a serving plate. Serve with cream.

PEAR AND CHESTNUT FLAN

*shortcrust pastry made with 150g, 6oz (1½ cups) plain
flour and 75g, 3oz (⅓ cup) margarine*

*225g, 8oz chestnut purée, sweetened
4 pears, peeled, cored and halved
25g, 1oz (¼ cup) flaked almonds*

Glaze

4 tbsp apple jelly

Roll out the pastry and use to line a greased 23cm (9in)
flan case. Prick the base and bake blind in the oven at gas
mark 5, 190°C (375°F) for 20 minutes. Allow to cool before spreading the chestnut purée over the base of the flan.
Arrange the pear halves over the purée. Cover with a glaze
of apple jelly. Heat the apple jelly gently in a small saucepan and then spread over the pears. To decorate, sprinkle
with flaked almonds.

PEAR AND BRAZIL NUT PIE

Brazil nuts are an excellent source of selenium, the antioxidant mineral which helps to protect against heart disease, ageing and cancer.

Pastry

100g, 4oz (1 cup) plain flour
100g, 4oz (1 cup) self-raising flour
50g, 2oz (⅓ cup) caster sugar
125g, 5oz (½ cup) butter, cut into pieces
50g, 2oz (½ cup) Brazil nuts, finely chopped
1 egg yolk
few drops vanilla essence
1 tbsp water

3 tbsp semolina
grated rind and juice of 1 lemon
25g, 1oz (⅛ cup) demerara sugar
900g, 2lb eating pears, peeled, cored and quartered
a little golden syrup

Sift the flours together. Add the sugar and butter, chopped Brazil nuts, egg yolk, vanilla essence and water. Work to a soft dough and then chill for 30 minutes. Roll out two thirds of the dough and use to line a greased, deep 20cm (8in) pie dish. Sprinkle half the semolina over the flan. Combine the remaining semolina with the lemon rind and juice and demerara sugar. Arrange the pears over the flan base. Spoon the lemon and semolina mixture over them. Roll out the remaining dough and place over the pears sealing the edges well. Bake in the oven at gas mark 6, 200°C (400°F) for 45 minutes. Glaze with the golden syrup before serving.

PEAR AND TOFFEE CRUMBLE

Dulce de Leche is a delicious caramel spread which you can buy in major supermarkets.

shortcrust pastry made with 150g, 6oz (1½ cups) plain flour and 75g, 3oz (⅓ cup) margarine

3 pears, peeled, cored and sliced
4 tbsp dulce de leche

Crumble topping

50g, 2oz (½ cup) light muscovado sugar
50g, 2oz (1 cup) porridge oats
25g, 1oz (¼ cup) plain flour
40g, 2½oz (¼ cup) butter

Roll out the shortcrust pastry and line a greased 20cm (8in) deep flan tin with it. Arrange the sliced pears over the pastry. Spoon the dulce de leche over the pears. To make the crumble topping, mix together the sugar, oats and flour and then rub in the butter. Spread this mixture over the pears and press down lightly. Bake in the oven at gas mark 4, 180°C (350°F) for about 40 minutes. Leave the pudding for at least an hour before serving, otherwise the dulce de leche will be too runny.

PEAR AND LEMON CRUMBLE

900g, 2lb pears, peeled, cored and sliced
3 tbsp golden syrup
grated rind of ½ lemon

Crumble topping

75g, 3oz (⅓ cup) butter or margarine
150g, 6oz (1½ cup) plain flour
75g, 3oz (½ cup) demerara sugar

Put the pears in a saucepan with two tablespoons of water and cook for 5 minutes. Place the pears and juices in a round baking dish and pour golden syrup over them. Sprinkle with the lemon rind. Rub the margarine or butter into the flour and stir in the sugar. Spoon the crumble over the pears. Cook in the oven at gas mark 4, 180°C (350°F) for about 30 minutes.

PEAR AND DAMSON CRUMBLE

Damsons cannot be eaten raw but are delicious cooked.

450g, 1lb damsons, halved and de-stoned
2 pears, cored, sliced and chopped
1 tbsp grated orange rind
50g, 2oz (⅓ cup) sugar

Topping

100g, 4oz (1 cup) plain flour
½ tsp cinnamon
75g, 3oz (⅓ cup) margarine
75g, 3oz (½ cup) demerara sugar
40g, 1½oz (¾ cup) porridge oats

Put the damsons and pears in a pie dish with the grated rind and sugar. Make the crumble topping by rubbing the margarine into the flour and cinnamon. Stir in the sugar and oats. Spread over the fruit mixture and bake in the oven at gas mark 5, 190°C (375°F) for 30 minutes.

PEAR AND PECAN UPSIDE DOWN PUDDING

This is a delicious, warming pudding for a cold
winter's evening.

75g, 3oz (⅓ cup) butter
150g, 6oz (1½ cups) light brown sugar
5 pears, peeled, cored and sliced
25g, 1oz (¼ cup) pecan nuts

Sponge

75g, 3oz (⅓ cup) butter
125g, 5oz (⅔ cup) caster sugar
100g, 4oz (1 cup) plain flour
2 tsp baking powder
¼ tsp cinnamon
¼ tsp ground nutmeg
2 eggs
150ml, ¼pt (⅔ cup) buttermilk or plain yoghurt

Melt the butter and mix in the brown sugar. Spread over
the base of a 23cm (9in) square cake tin. Arrange the sliced
pears over the base and tuck the pecan nuts in between the
pears. To make the sponge, beat together the butter and
sugar. Sieve the dry ingredients together. Lightly beat the
eggs and gradually add them to the butter mixture. Fold in
the dry ingredients alternately with spoonfuls of the buttermilk. When everything is well combined pour the mixture over the pears and pecans. Cook in the oven at gas
mark 4, 180°C (350°F) for 40 minutes.

STEAMED PEAR PUDDING

This is similar to a treacle pudding but the pear and lemon give it an extra flavour. Children will love it.

3 tbsp golden syrup
150g, 6oz (1½ cup) self-raising flour
1 tsp baking powder
100g, 4oz (½ cup) butter or margarine
100g, 4oz (⅔ cup) golden caster sugar
2 eggs
2 pears, peeled, cored and diced
grated rind of 1 lemon
single cream, to serve

Spoon the golden syrup into the bottom of a 1.1litre, 2pt pudding basin and spread some of the syrup up the sides of the basin. Combine the flour, baking powder, butter or margarine, sugar and eggs in a food processor and process until everything is mixed together. Fold in the diced pears and the lemon rind. Spoon into the pudding basin. Cover with greaseproof paper making a pleat in the centre and secure with a rubber band. Place in a steamer and cover with a lid. Steam for 2 hours. Invert the pudding onto a serving plate and serve if liked with a little extra warmed golden syrup or with single cream.

PEAR AND GINGER
SPONGE PUDDING

This is a simple sponge with pears underneath.

450g, 1lb pears, peeled, cored and sliced
50g, 2oz (½ cup) light brown sugar
½ tsp ground ginger

Sponge

100g, 4oz (½ cup) margarine
100g, 4oz (⅔ cup) caster sugar
100g, 4oz (1 cup) self-raising flour
1 tsp ground ginger
2 eggs

Arrange the pear slices in a greased ovenproof dish. Sprinkle evenly with the sugar and ground ginger. Make the sponge by combining the margarine, sugar, eggs and flour, sifted with the ginger. You can mix everything together using an electric whisk. Spoon over the fruit. Bake in the oven at gas mark 5, 190°C (375°F) for 25 minutes. Serve warm with cream or custard.

PEAR AND BLACKBERRY
SPONGE PUDDING

Pears and blackberries go rather well together and so this makes a nice healthy autumn pudding.

Sponge base

100g, 4oz (½ cup) butter
50g, 2oz (⅓ cup) caster sugar
50g, 2oz (½ cup) self-raising flour
50g, 2oz (½ cup) wholemeal self-raising flour
1 egg

Filling

450g, 1lb pears, peeled, cored and halved
100g, 4oz blackberries, washed
150ml, ¼pt (⅔ cup) soured cream
1 egg
½ tsp vanilla essence
50g, 2oz (⅓ cup) golden caster sugar

Combine all the ingredients for the sponge together in a food processor and process until blended. Spoon into the base of a greased 20cm (8in) square cake tin. Arrange the halved pears and blackberries over the sponge. Beat the cream, egg, vanilla essence and sugar together and pour over the top. Bake in the oven at gas mark 5, 190°C (375°F) for about 30 minutes. The filling will set as the pudding cools.

PEAR BREAD AND BUTTER PUDDING

225g, 8oz white bread, sliced and buttered
5 pears, peeled, cored and quartered
100g, 4oz (1cup) light brown sugar
pinch of ground nutmeg
2 eggs
300ml, ½pt (1¼ cups) milk

Cover the base and sides of a greased ovenproof dish with the buttered slices of bread. Place the pear quarters over the bread and sprinkle on most of the sugar and nutmeg. Cover with a layer of bread and sprinkle on remaining sugar. Whisk the eggs and mix in the milk. Pour over the bread mixture, pressing the bread down into the milk. Sprinkle any remaining sugar over the top. Bake in the oven at gas mark 4, 180°C (350°F) for about 1 hour by which time the pudding should be golden brown.

PEAR SURPRISE PUDDING

A great family pudding. Children love finding the hidden pears under the lemon pudding.

450g, 1lb pears, peeled, cored and sliced
15g, ½oz (1 tbsp) butter
100g, 4oz (⅔ cup) granulated sugar
2 eggs, spearated
grated rind and juice of 1 lemon
1 tbsp flour
150ml, ¼pt (⅔ cup) milk

Place the pears in the bottom of an ovenproof dish. Beat the butter into the granulated sugar. Beat in the egg yolks, the lemon rind and juice, the flour and the milk. Whisk the egg whites and gently fold into the lemon mixture. Pour this on top of the pears. Stand the tin in a roasting tin half full of water and bake in the oven at gas mark 4, 180°C (350°F) for 30 minutes.

REDCURRANT AND PEAR COBBLER

½ tsp cinnamon
¼ tsp nutmeg
1 tsp cornflour
150ml, ¼pt (⅔ cup) water
225g, 8oz redcurrants
100g, 4oz (⅔ cup) sugar
2 large pears, peeled, cored and sliced
150g, 6oz (1½ cups) wholemeal flour
1 tsp baking powder
40g, 1½oz (3 tbsp) melted butter
1 egg
150ml, ¼pt (⅔ cup) soured cream
cream, to serve

Mix the spices and cornflour and gradually add the water to make a smooth paste. Put the redcurrants and 50g, 2oz (⅓ cup) of the sugar in a saucepan, add the liquid paste and bring gradually to the boil and simmer for 3 minutes. Put the pears in an ovenproof dish and pour over the redcurrant mixture. Meanwhile mix the flour, the rest of the sugar and the baking powder in a bowl. Add the melted butter, egg and soured cream and mix together. Drop spoonfuls of this mixture over the pears and redcurrants until they are almost entirely covered. Bake in the oven at gas mark 5, 190°C (375°F) for 30 minutes. Serve hot with cream.

BATTER FLAN WITH PEARS AND PLUMS

Batter

1 egg
150ml, ¼pt (⅔ cup) milk
1 tbsp honey
75g, 3oz (⅔ cup) plain flour

225g, 8oz pears, cored and sliced
225g, 8oz red plums, de-stoned and halved
dusting of icing sugar

For the batter put the egg, milk and honey in a food processor and blend. Add the flour and process again. Grease a 23cm (9in) flan dish. Pour the batter in and put the pears and plums on top, letting them sink in. Bake in the oven at gas mark 6, 200°C (400°F) for 40 minutes. The flan will be brown and the fruit soft. Dust with icing sugar before serving.

PEAR AND ALMOND FRITTERS

Batter

75g, 3oz (¾ cup) plain flour
1 egg, separated
1 tbsp oil
2 tbsp milk
2 tbsp water

4 pears, peeled, cored and halved
4 tbsp ground almonds
1 tbsp caster sugar
25g, 1oz (2 tbsp) butter
oil for deep frying

Sift the flour into a bowl and break in the egg yolk. Add the oil and gradually pour in the milk and water. Stir everything together until well combined. Whisk the egg white and fold into the batter. Mix together the almonds, sugar and butter. Press a little mixture into the centre of each pear half. Dip each pear half into the batter and deep fry for a few minutes until golden brown. Serve at once and dust with extra caster sugar, if desired.

PEAR CHEESECAKE

shortcrust pastry made with 150g, 6oz (1½ cups) plain
flour and 75g, 3oz (⅓ cup) margarine

225g, 8oz curd cheese
few drops of vanilla essence
125ml, 4 fl oz (½ cup) plain yoghurt
1 egg, beaten
450g, 1lb pears, Comice or Williams, peeled,
cored and quartered

Roll out two thirds of the pastry and line a greased, deep 20cm (8in) flan dish. Beat together the cheese, vanilla essence, yoghurt and egg. Pour the cheese mixture into the flan case. Arrange the pear quarters on top and press them in lightly. Roll out the remaining pastry and cut into strips. Use to make a lattice design over the pear and cheese mixture. Bake the flan in the oven at gas mark 3, 160°C (325°F) for 1 hour. Leave to cool in the oven and serve cold.

CHOCOLATE AND PEAR
MERINGUE PIE

Pastry

100g, 4oz (1 cup) plain flour
25g, 1oz (⅓ cup) cocoa powder
75g, 3oz (⅓ cup) margarine

Filling

3 ripe pears, peeled, cored and quartered
2 egg whites
100g, 4oz (⅔ cup) caster sugar
2 tbsp cocoa powder
cream to serve

To make the pastry, mix together the flour and cocoa powder, rub in the margarine and mix to a dough with a little cold water. Roll out the pastry and use to line a greased 20cm (8in) flan case. Prick the pastry and bake the flan blind in the oven at gas mark 5, 190°C (375°F) for 10 minutes. Arrange the pear quarters over the flan. Whisk the egg whites until stiff and then whisk in the sugar. Fold in the cocoa powder and spoon the mixture over the pears. Bake in the oven at gas mark 5, 190°C (375°F) for 30 minutes. Serve warm with cream.

PEAR AND RASPBERRY PAVLOVA

Meringue

4 egg whites
225g, 8oz (1 ⅓ cups) caster sugar
½ tbsp cornflour, sifted
1 tsp vinegar
1 tsp vanilla essence

Topping

150ml, ¼pt (⅔ cup) whipping cream
150ml, ¼pt (⅔ cup) soured cream
225g, 8oz raspberries
225g, 8oz pears, peeled, cored and sliced
50g, 2oz (⅓ cup) sugar

To make the pavlova, beat the egg whites until stiff. Gradually beat in the sugar, a little at a time. Sprinkle the cornflour, vinegar and vanilla over the mixture and fold in carefully. Make a circle with the meringue mixture on a large greased baking sheet. Bake for 1 hour at gas mark 1, 120°C (275°F). The pavlova should be crisp on the outside with a soft marshmallow centre. Whip the cream with the soured cream. Spread this over the meringue. Cook the raspberries with the sugar over a gentle heat until the juices run. Add the pears and cook for a couple more minutes. Carefully pour the pear slices and raspberries over the cream and serve at once.

PEARS ARMANDINE

Pears and strawberries work well together and this is a
light, healthy pudding. The sieved strawberries over the
pears add a lovely colour to this dessert.

300ml, ½pt (1¼ cups) water
100g, 4oz (⅔ cup) sugar
1 tsp vanilla essence
4 pears, peeled, halved and cored
25g, 1oz (¼ cup) flaked almonds
225g, 8oz strawberries
cream, to serve

Boil the sugar and water for a few minutes. Add the vanilla
essence and poach the pears in this syrup until they are just
tender. Turn over every so often. Put them in a serving
dish and stick the almonds into the sides of the pears. Boil
the syrup to reduce by half. Add the strawberries and boil
for a few minutes. Sieve the strawberries and spoon over
the pears. Chill and serve with cream.

PEAR MOUSSE

This is a light pudding and suitable for slimmers.

100g, 4oz dried pears, soaked overnight
100g, 4oz curd cheese
1 tbsp lemon juice
1 egg white
1 tbsp clear honey
1 fresh pear, sliced thinly to decorate

Cook the dried pears in 450ml, ¾pt (1½ cups) of the soaking liquid for 30 minutes. Drain, reserving 2 tablespoons of the liquid. Cool and then place in a food processor with the reserved liquid and blend with the cheese and 2 teaspoons of the lemon juice. Whisk the egg white until stiff, then whisk in the honey. Fold the egg white into the pear mixture and spoon into a serving bowl. Decorate with the pear slices and brush with the remaining lemon juice.

PEARS BELLE HÉLÈNE

This is a traditional pear pudding - chocolate, pears and ice cream - what a delicious combination.

Vanilla ice cream

4 eggs, separated
100g, 4oz (1 cup) icing sugar, sieved
few drops of vanilla essence
300ml, ½pt (1¼ cups) double cream

6 pears, peeled, cored and halved

Chocolate fudge sauce

25g, 1oz plain chocolate
15g, ½oz butter
1 small can evaporated milk
50g, 2oz (⅓ cup) soft brown sugar
2 tbsp golden syrup

To make the ice cream, whip the egg yolks with half of the sieved icing sugar until the mixture is pale and very thick. Whisk in the vanilla essence. Whisk the double cream until thick. Whisk the egg whites until they are stiff. Gradually add the sieved icing sugar and keep whisking until the mixture is very stiff. Fold the egg yolk mixture into the cream and then add the egg white mixture. Pour into a freezer container and freeze. To make the sauce put all the ingredients in a saucepan and heat gently until melted. Bring to the boil, then lower the heat and simmer for 5 minutes by which time the sauce should be thick and glossy. Arrange the pears round the ice cream in a dish or on separate plates and pour over the chocolate sauce.

PEAR ICE CREAM

This delicious ice cream would go well with a compôte
of red berries.

*450g, 1lb sweet pears, either Comice or Williams,
peeled, cored and sliced
50g, 2oz (¼ cup) butter
25g, 1oz (1 tbsp) sugar
1 tbsp elderflower syrup
strip of lemon peel
2 egg yolks
300ml, ½pt (1¼ cups) crème fraîche*

Cook the pear slices gently with the butter, sugar,
elderflower syrup, lemon peel and 4 tablespoons of water
in a saucepan until soft. Remove the peel and purée the
fruit. Beat in the egg yolks and cook over a low heat until
the mixture thickens, stirring constantly. Leave to cool, stirring every so often. Pour the mixture into a container and
freeze for about an hour. Whip the crème fraîche and fold
into the half-frozen pear mixture. Cover and freeze until
firm.

PEAR SORBET

*3 large ripe pears, preferably Williams, peeled, cored
and sliced
150ml, ¼pt (⅔ cup) good quality sweet white wine
75g, 3oz (½ cup) sugar
piece of lemon peel*

Poach the pears with the wine, sugar and lemon peel for
about 5 minutes. Leave to cool. Remove the lemon peel
and purée the pear mixture. Pour into a freezer container
and freeze, beating twice at 45 minute intervals. Transfer
the sorbet to the fridge about 15 minutes before serving.

TEA-TIME TREATS

PEAR MUFFINS

225g, 8oz (2 cups) self-raising flour
100g, 4oz(⅔ cup) caster sugar
100g, 4oz (½ cup) butter
2 eggs
125ml, 4 fl oz (½ cup) milk
1 tsp vanilla essence
225g, 8oz pears, peeled, cored and chopped
1 tbsp caster sugar
¼ tsp nutmeg

Beat together the flour, sugar, butter, eggs, milk and vanilla essence either in a food processor or with an electric whisk. Fold in the pears until evenly combined. Pat spoonfuls of the mixture into greased muffin tins and sprinkle with the caster sugar and a little nutmeg. Bake in the oven for 15 minutes at gas mark 6, 200°C (400°F). Leave in the tin for a few minutes before turning out. Serve warm with butter and jam.

PEAR SHORTCAKE

A simple but quite wholesome tea-time treat.

150g, 6oz (1½ cup) plain wholemeal flour
100g, 4oz (½ cups) margarine
50g, 2oz (½ cup) soft brown sugar
few drops of vanilla essence
75g, 3oz curd cheese
1 tbsp honey
2 pears, peeled, cored and chopped

Grease a baking sheet. Rub the margarine into the flour and stir in the sugar and the vanilla essence. Knead lightly with your hands and then roll out into a circle. Place on the baking sheet. Bake in the oven at gas mark 3, 160°C (325°F) for 30 minutes. Mix together the curd cheese and the honey. Add the chopped pears. Spread this mixture over the shortbread and cut into slices before serving.

PEAR AND LEMON SPONGE

2 large pears, peeled, cored and chopped
2 tbsp soured cream
2 eggs
grated rind of 2 lemons
1 tsp vanilla essence
125g, 5oz (⅔ cup) butter
150g, 6oz (1 cup) caster sugar
175g, 7oz (1¾ cups) plain flour
1 tsp bicarbonate of soda

Topping

juice of 2 lemons
75g, 3oz (½ cup) sugar

Put the pears, soured cream, eggs, lemon rind and vanilla essence into a bowl and beat together. Cream together the butter and sugar, and gradually add the flour, bicarbonate of soda and the pear mixture. Pour into a greased 23cm (9in) cake tin and cook for about 50 minutes at gas mark 4, 180°C (350°F). For the topping, melt the sugar in the lemon juice over a gentle heat and pour over the cake when you take it out of the oven. Leave to cool in the tin before serving.

PEAR AND NUTMEG FLAPJACKS

125g, 5oz (1¼ cups) self-raising flour
150g, 6oz (3 cups) porridge oats
175g, 7oz (1¾ cups) soft brown sugar
1 tsp nutmeg
175g, 7oz (¾ cup) margarine, melted
2 large firm pears, peeled, cored and sliced

Combine flour, oats, sugar and nutmeg. Then add the melted margarine and mix thoroughly. Put half the mixture into a greased 27.5 x 17.5cm (11 x 7in) baking tin and press down. Cover with sliced pears and then with the rest of the mixture. It may be quite difficult to spread this on top of the pears. It might help to use a spatula or the flat of your hands. Bake in the oven at gas mark 4, 180°C (350°F) for 25 minutes. Allow to cool before cutting into slices.

PEAR AND ALMOND CAKE

75g, 3oz (⅓ cup) butter, softened
75g, 3oz (½ cup) caster sugar
3 eggs, beaten
100g, 4 oz (1 cup) self-raising flour
125g, 5oz (1¼ cups) ground almonds
1 tsp almond essence
450g, 1lb pears, peeled, cored and halved

Beat the butter and sugar together. Gradually add the eggs along with the flour and almonds. Beat in the almond essence. Pour the mixture into a greased 23cm (9in) cake tin and arrange the pear halves over the surface. Bake in the oven at gas mark 4, 180°C (350°F) for 40 minutes.

PEAR AND ALMOND GINGERBREAD

2 pears, peeled, cored and diced
juice of ½ lemon
100g, 4oz (½ cup) butter
100g, 4oz (⅔ cup) sugar
2 eggs, beaten
2 tbsp black treacle
175g, 7oz (1¾ cups) plain flour
2 tbsp ground almonds
1 tsp ginger
1 tsp mixed spice
1 tsp bicarbonate of soda
300ml, ½pt (1¼ cups) milk, warmed

Soak the diced pear in the lemon juice. Cream butter and sugar and gradually beat in the eggs. Stir in the treacle. Mix the bicarbonate into the warmed milk. Sieve the remaining dry ingredients and add alternately with the milk to the creamed mixture. Finally fold in the pieces of pear. Grease a 27.5 x 17.5cm (11 x 7in) baking tin and fill with the mixture. Bake in the oven at gas mark 4, 180°C (350°F) for 45 minutes. Serve warm or cold dredged with icing sugar.

PRESERVES

SPICED PEARS

900g, 2lb firm pears, peeled, cored and quartered
450g, 1lb (3 cups) sugar
300ml, ½pt (1¼ cups) malt vinegar
8 cloves
2 tsp allspice
1 stick of cinnamon

Put the sugar and vinegar into a saucepan and add the spices tied up in a piece of muslin. Stir over a low heat to dissolve the sugar, add the pears and bring to the boil. Simmer until the pears are tender. Life the pears out of the syrup and transfer to a jar. Remove the bag of spices. Return the syrup to the heat and boil until it is thick. Pour it over the pears and seal. Store for a month before using.

PEAR AND GINGER CHUTNEY

Makes 2 - 3 jars

1kg, 2lb pears, peeled, cored and chopped
3 large onions, peeled and chopped
75g, 3oz (¾ cup) raisins
2 tbsp fresh root ginger, chopped
150g, 6oz (1 cup) dark brown sugar
300ml, ½pt (1¼ cups) vinegar
1 stick of cinnamon

Put the pears and onions in a large saucepan with the raisins. Add the ginger, sugar, vinegar and cinnamon and bring slowly to the boil, stirring every so often. Reduce the heat and simmer, uncovered for about 1 hour. Stir occasionally to prevent the chutney sticking to the pan. Spoon the chutney into warm jars and leave for a couple of weeks before using.

PEAR AND LEMON CHUTNEY

Makes 4 - 5 jars

1.8kg, 4lb pears, peeled, cored and chopped
450g, 1lb onions, skinned and chopped
350g, 12oz (3 cups) raisins
50g, 2oz stem ginger, chopped
grated rind and juice of 2 lemons
225g, 8oz (1 ⅓ cups) brown sugar
2 tsp salt
1.1l, 2 pts (5 cups) vinegar
2 cloves of garlic, skinned and crushed
6 dried red chillies, crushed
4 cloves

Place the pears, onions, raisins, ginger, lemon rind and juice, sugar, salt and vinegar in a large saucepan. Tie the garlic, chillies and cloves in a muslin bag. Add to the pan. Bring to the boil and simmer gently for about 2 hours until thick. Remove the muslin bag, pot and seal.

PEAR AND PEPPER CHUTNEY

Makes 5 jars

1.8kg, 4lb pears, peeled, cored and chopped
450g, 1lb onions, peeled and chopped
450g, 1lb tomatoes, skinned and chopped
2 green peppers, seeds removed and chopped
450g, 1lb (3 cups) demerara sugar
225g, 8oz (2 cups) raisins
2 cloves of garlic, peeled and crushed
a pinch of cayenne pepper
1 tsp ground ginger
850ml, 1½pts (3¾ cups) spiced pickling vinegar

Place the pears, onions and tomatoes in a large saucepan and cook for about 20 minutes. Then add all the remaining ingredients and cook for about 1½ hours until the chutney is thick. Stir every so often to prevent the chutney sticking to the bottom of the pan. Spoon into warm screw-top jars and store for at least a month before using.

PEAR JAM

Makes 3 - 4 jars

1.4kg, 3lb firm pears, chopped (reserve peel and cores)
juice and rind of 1 large lemon
150ml, ¼pt (⅔ cup) water
600g, 1lb 5oz (4 cups) jam sugar

Put the pear cores and peel in a saucepan with the lemon rind and water and boil for 10 minutes. Strain and return the liquid to the pan with the chopped pear and lemon juice. Simmer gently until the pears are tender. Add the sugar, stir over a low heat until dissolved, and bring to the boil. Boil until setting point is reached. Pot and seal.

PEAR AND BLACKBERRY JAM

Makes 7 jars

900g, 2lb blackberries
1.4kg, 3lb pears, chopped (reserve peel and cores)
juice and grated rind of 3 lemons (reserve pips)
1 stick of cinnamon
1.8kg, 4lb (12 cups) jam sugar

Put the blackberries, pears, lemon rind and juice in a large saucepan. Put the reserved pips, pear cores and peel in a muslin bag and add to the pan. Heat gently and simmer for 20 minutes. Remove the muslin. Add the sugar and stir to dissolve. Bring to the boil and boil rapidly until setting point is reached. Pot and seal.

APPLES

STARTERS

APPLE AND MUSHROOM SOUP

Serves 8

100g, 4oz (½ cup) butter
225g, 8oz onions, peeled and chopped
450g, 1lb apples, chopped
450g, 1lb mushrooms, washed and chopped
150ml, ¼pt (⅔ cup) sherry
900ml, 1½pt (3 cups) vegetable stock
salt and pepper
2 tbsp thick cream
1 tbsp chives, chopped

Cook the chopped onions in the butter in a large saucepan over a low heat for about 10 minutes. Add the chopped apple (unpeeled) and the mushrooms. Pour in the sherry and stir well. Cover with a lid and simmer for 40 minutes. Add the stock. Then put the soup in a food processor and process, before passing through a sieve to get rid of any stalk or skin from the apples. Add seasoning to taste, and reheat slowly over a low heat. Serve with a dollop of cream and some snipped chives.

PINK SOUP

Serves 6

50g, 2oz (¼ cup) butter
1 onion, peeled and chopped
2 cooking apples, peeled, cored and chopped
25g, 1oz (¼ cup) plain flour
1.2l, 2pts (5 cups) chicken stock
1 small tin of sweetcorn
300ml, ½pt (1¼ cups) single cream
100g, 4oz cooked beetroot, chopped

Fry the onion in the butter in a large saucepan until soft. Add the chopped apple. Stir in the flour and gradually stir in the chicken stock. Bring to the boil and stir. Add the sweetcorn, cover the pan and simmer for 15 minutes. Cool slightly and blend in a food processor until it is as smooth as possible. Pass the mixture through a sieve. Add the cream. Reheat the soup and stir in the beetroot. As you stir in the beetroot the soup will become pink. Serve at once.

CUCUMBER AND APPLE SOUP

Serves 4 - 6

450g, 1lb cooking apples, peeled, cored and sliced
grated rind and juice of 1 lemon
2 cucumbers, peeled
1 small clove of garlic, peeled and crushed
1 glass white wine
sea salt and pepper
150ml, ¼pt (⅔ cup) soured cream

Cook the apples in a little water with lemon rind and juice. Purée. Grate in the cucumber, removing any large seeds. Sprinkle with salt and leave for a couple of hours. Add the crushed garlic and wine, and stir. Chill and serve with a dollop of soured cream added to each bowl of soup.

CARROT SOUP WITH
CREAMED APPLE

Serves 4

25g, 1oz (2 tbsp) butter
2 onions, peeled and chopped
2 tsp curry powder
450g, 1lb carrots, peeled and chopped
1 slice of lemon
1.2l, 2 pts (5 cups) chicken stock
salt and pepper

Apple Sauce

450g, 1lb cooking apples, peeled, cored and sliced
1 tbsp sugar
60ml, 2fl oz (¼ cup) water
60ml, 2fl oz (¼ cup) double cream

Cook the onion in the butter in a saucepan. Stir in the curry powder and cook for a couple of minutes. Add the carrots, lemon, chicken stock and seasoning. Bring to the boil and then reduce the heat and simmer covered for 30 minutes. To make the creamed apple, place the apples, sugar and water in a saucepan and cook for about 10 minutes. Cool and purée. Whip the cream and fold into the apple purée. Cool the soup before placing in a food processor and blending until smooth. Reheat and serve hot with the creamed apple served separately.

CARAMELISED APPLE
AND STILTON SALAD

Serves 4

50g, 2oz (¼ cup) butter
1 tbsp caster sugar
2 eating apples, Discovery or Royal Gala,
cored and sliced
1 bunch of mixed lettuce leaves
100g, 4oz Blue Stilton cheese
chopped fresh herbs (mint, parsley, rosemary, thyme or
basil)

Dressing

4 tbsp olive oil
2 tbsp red wine vinegar
salt and pepper

Heat the butter in a frying pan and fry the apple slices with the sugar until they begin to caramelise. Remove from the pan and cool. Arrange the lettuce in a serving bowl and crumble the stilton on top. Add the apple slices and fresh herbs. Combine the oil, vinegar and seasoning and pour over the salad.

BACON AND APPLE SALAD

Serves 4

225g, 8oz streaky bacon, fried and chopped
225g, 8oz eating apples, peeled, cored and diced
100g, 4oz radishes, sliced
4 tbsp mayonnaise
1 tbsp lemon juice
1 bunch of watercress

Combine the bacon, apple, radishes and mayonnaise. Add the lemon juice. Serve on a bed of watercress.

PRAWN, APPLE AND RADICCHIO SALAD

Serves 3-4

100g, 4oz radicchio leaves
225g, 8oz prawns
225g, 8oz green eating apples, Granny Smiths or
Braeburns, cored and sliced
4 tbsp apple juice
1 tsp chopped mint
1 tsp vinegar

Mix together the prawns and apples. Lay over the radicchio leaves. Pour the apple juice over them. Mix together the vinegar and mint and sprinkle over the apples and prawns.

MANGE TOUT AND APPLE SALAD WITH TOASTED HAZELNUTS

This makes a healthy refreshing salad.

Serves 4

350g, 12oz mange tout
2 Cox's apples, cored and chopped
50g, 2oz toasted hazelnuts

Dressing

4 tbsp olive oil
2 tbsp hazelnut oil
2 tbsp cider vinegar
salt and pepper
1 tsp grain mustard

Blanch the mange tout in boiling water for a couple of minutes. Drain and run cold water over them to keep them green. Put in a serving bowl with the chopped apples. Make the dressing by combining the oils, vinegar, mustard and seasoning. Pour over the apple and mange tout. Chop the hazelnuts and scatter over the salad. Serve at once.

MAIN DISHES

Mackerel with Cider and Apples   79
White Fish with Apples   80
Pork Chops with Red Cabbage and Apple   81
Pork in Pastry   82
Pork with Parsnip and Apple   83
Bacon Steaks with Cucumber and Apple Sauce   84
Chicken and Apple Parcels   85
Chicken and Apple Curry   86
Veal Escalopes with Apple and Okra   87
Pheasant with Juniper and Apples   88
Stilton and Apple Stuffed Onions   89
Cheese and Apple Bake   90
Apple and Ham Bake   91
Fennel and Apple Gratin   92
Apple and Lime Rosti   93
Chestnut, Apple and Prune Casserole   94

MACKEREL WITH
CIDER AND APPLES

Serves 4

*4 small mackerel, gutted with heads and
backbones removed
salt and pepper
1 onion, peeled and sliced
1 eating apple, peeled, cored and sliced
1 tbsp lemon juice
a few peppercorns
2 bay leaves
300ml, ½pt (1¼ cups) cider*

Season the mackerel with salt and pepper and place in a shallow ovenproof dish. Spread the onion slices around the fish. Toss the apple in the lemon juice and add to the dish with the peppercorns and bay leaves. Pour over the cider and cover. Cook in the oven at gas mark 4, 180°C (350°F) for 30 minutes.

WHITE FISH WITH APPLES

Serves 4

4 white fish fillets
seasoned flour
50g, 2oz (¼ cup) butter
2 tbsp sunflower oil
2 eating apples, peeled, cored and sliced
juice of ½ lemon
pepper

Dip the fish in the flour. Melt 25g, 1oz (2 tbsp) of the butter with the oil in a large frying pan. Fry the fish for 10 minutes. Arrange on a serving dish and keep warm. Fry the apples in the remaining butter in a clean frying pan and add the lemon juice and pepper. Fry until the apples are soft and then spoon over the fish.

PORK CHOPS WITH RED CABBAGE AND APPLE

Serves 4

1 small red cabbage, shredded
1 onion, peeled and sliced
4 cloves
1 eating apple, Cox or Discovery, cored and sliced
4 tbsp red wine vinegar
4 tbsp demerara sugar
salt and pepper
4 pork chops
2 tbsp sunflower oil
150ml, ¼pt (⅔ cup) red wine
100g, 4oz cranberries

Put the cabbage, onion, cloves, apple, vinegar, sugar and seasoning in a casserole and cook in the oven at gas mark 4, 180°C (350°F) for 1 hour. Fry the pork chops on both sides in the oil. Add the red wine, cranberries and salt and pepper. Cover and simmer gently for about 30 minutes. Serve the pork chops accompanied by the cabbage and apple.

PORK IN PASTRY

Serves 3 - 4

450g, 1lb pork fillet
3 tbsp sunflower oil
15g, ½oz (1 tbsp) butter
1 onion, peeled and chopped
4 rashers of unsmoked streaky bacon, chopped
75g, 3oz mushrooms
1 cooking apple, peeled, cored and chopped
sprinkling of mixed herbs
salt and pepper
150g, 6oz packet of frozen puff pastry, thawed
beaten egg to glaze
1 tbsp flour
300ml, ½pt (1¼ cups) beef stock
1 tbsp tomato purée

Fry the pork fillets in the oil in a frying pan until brown all over. Keep the juices for the gravy. Fry the onion and bacon in the butter in a saucepan. Add the mushrooms and apple, herbs and seasoning and fry for a few minutes. Roll out the pastry. Spread the apple and onion mixture down the centre of the pastry and place the pork on top. Wrap the pastry around the pork and seal, dampening with water. Place in a greased baking tin with the seal underneath and cook in the oven at gas mark 5, 190°C (375°F) for 50 minutes. Cover with greaseproof paper if the pastry is in danger of getting too brown. Now make the gravy. Stir the flour into the reserved juices from the frying pan that you cooked the pork in. Gradually add the stock and tomato purée and bring to the boil. Simmer for a couple of minutes. Season. Serve the pork with the gravy.

PORK WITH PARSNIP AND APPLE

This is a good, wholesome, tasty pork casserole.

Serves 3 - 4

3 tbsp olive oil
450g, 1lb pork fillet, cubed
1 onion, peeled and chopped
3 tbsp plain wholemeal flour
2 medium parsnips, peeled and chopped
225g, 8oz cooking apples, peeled, cored and chopped
450ml, ¾pt (1½ cups) dry cider
½ tsp mustard powder
½ tsp dried thyme
2 tsp tarragon
1 tsp Worcestershire sauce
1 tsp chopped parsley
salt and pepper

Heat the oil in a casserole, add the pork and brown on all sides. Remove the pork from the casserole and add the onion. Fry until soft. Stir in the flour and cook for a couple of minutes. Add the parsnips and fry for a couple more minutes. Return the pork to the casserole with the apple and pour over the cider. Bring to the boil and stir until thickened. Stir in the mustard powder, herbs and Worcestershire sauce. Add the salt and pepper, cover and cook in the oven at gas mark 4, 180°C (350°F) for 45 minutes.

BACON STEAKS WITH CUCUMBER
AND APPLE SAUCE

Serves 4

4 bacon steaks
25g, 1oz (2 tbsp) butter, melted

Sauce

half a cucumber, diced
1 eating apple, Braeburn or Royal Gala, peeled, cored
and diced
15g, ½oz (1 tbsp) butter
15g, ½oz (2 tbsp) flour
300ml, ½pt (1¼ cups) milk
2 tbsp double cream
1 tbsp chives, chopped
pinch of cayenne pepper

Brush the bacon steaks with the melted butter and grill for 5 minutes on each side. Make the sauce by cooking the diced cucumber in boiling, salted water for 3 minutes. Drain thoroughly. Melt the butter, add the flour and stir over a low heat. Gradually pour in the milk stirring all the time, and bring the sauce to the boil. Add seasoning and a pinch of cayenne and then the cucumber, apple, cream and chives. Stir for a minute or two over the heat and spoon over the bacon steaks when you serve them.

CHICKEN AND APPLE PARCELS

Serves 4

4 skinless chicken breasts
2 eating apples, peeled, cored and sliced
8 rashers unsmoked streaky bacon
1 tbsp sunflower oil
1 clove of garlic, peeled and crushed
225g, 8oz mushrooms
300ml, ½pt (1¼ cups) cider
1 tsp cornflour mixed to a paste with a little water
salt and pepper
parsley

Flatten the chicken breasts using a rolling pin. Place slices of the apple in the centre of each chicken breast and roll up. Wrap each one with 2 rashers of bacon and secure with cocktail sticks. Place the breasts in a large frying pan with the garlic and fry for 10 minutes until brown on each side. Add the mushrooms and cook for a further 5 minutes. Then add the cider and simmer for 10 minutes. Add salt and pepper. Remove the breasts and add the cornflour paste to the juices. Stir until thickened. Pour the sauce over the chicken and sprinkle with parsley.

CHICKEN AND APPLE CURRY

Serves 4 - 6

4 large chicken joints
flour
25g, 1oz (2 tbsp) butter

Sauce

40g, 1½oz (3 tbsp) butter
1 onion, chopped
1 cooking apple, peeled, cored and diced
3 tbsp curry powder
600ml, 1pt (2½ cups) chicken stock
bay leaf
1 tbsp mango chutney
1 tbsp brown sugar
juice of ½ lemon
salt
1 tbsp cornflour mixed to a paste with 2 tbsp cold water

Sprinkle flour over the chicken joints. Melt the butter in a frying pan and fry the chicken until brown. Put in a casserole. To prepare the sauce, melt the butter in a saucepan and add the onion and apple. Cook for a couple of minutes, then add the curry powder, stir in the stock and bring to the boil. Add the bay leaf, chutney, sugar, lemon juice and salt. Pour over the chicken in the casserole, cover with a lid and cook in the oven at gas mark 4, 180°C (350°F) for 1 hour. Lift the chicken out, add the cornflour paste and stir until the sauce thickens. Pour the sauce over the chicken and serve with rice.

VEAL ESCALOPES
WITH APPLE AND OKRA

Serves 4

4 veal escalopes
flour
75g, 3oz full fat soft cheese
1 egg, beaten
50g, 2oz (½ cup) white breadcrumbs
4 tbsp olive oil
350g, 12oz okra, trimmed
200ml, 7fl oz (¾ cup) apple juice
2 green eating apples, peeled, cored and sliced
1 tbsp cider vinegar

Flatten the veal by pounding with a rolling pin. Coat in flour. Spread the cream cheese over two of the escalopes. Place the other escalopes on top and press down. Slice into strips. Coat in more flour and dip into the beaten egg and then coat with breadcrumbs. Fry the veal strips in the olive oil in a casserole until golden brown. Remove with a slotted spoon. Add the okra and fry them for a few minutes. Add the apple juice and simmer, covered for about 10 minutes. Stir in the apple slices and vinegar. Return the veal strips to the casserole and heat for a few minutes. Serve at once.

PHEASANT WITH JUNIPER BERRIES AND APPLES

Serves 6

225g, 8oz streaky bacon, chopped
2 tbsp juniper berries, crushed
2 pheasants
4 tbsp brandy
225g, 8oz pickling onions, peeled
2 celery sticks, sliced
bay leaf
salt and pepper
4 tbsp flour
1 bottle red wine
4 Cox's apples, cored and sliced
25g, 1oz (2 tbsp) butter

Fry the bacon in a large frying pan. Remove the bacon and set aside. Add the juniper berries, cook for a minute, then add the pheasants and cook until brown all over. Place the birds in a large casserole and sprinkle the bacon and juniper berries over them. Warm the brandy in a small saucepan and pour over the birds. Set the brandy alight. Add the onions, celery and bay leaf to the frying pan and cook for a few minutes. Stir in the salt and pepper and the flour and gradually pour in the wine, stirring all the time. Bring to the boil and then pour into the casserole. Cook the casserole with the lid on in the oven at gas mark 4, 180°C (350°F) for 1½ hours. Meanwhile, fry the apple slices in the butter in a frying pan to brown them and add to the casserole just before serving.

STILTON AND APPLE STUFFED ONIONS

This makes an excellent veggie meal. Serve with crusty
brown bread.

Serves 4

4 large onions, peeled
225g, 8oz cooking apples, peeled, cored and chopped
100g, 4oz (1 cup) fresh breadcrumbs
100g, 4oz Blue Stilton cheese, crumbled
1 bunch watercress, chopped
50g, 2oz (¼ cup) butter

Cook the onions in a large saucepan of boiling water for
15 minutes. Drain and allow to cool. Mix the chopped
apples with the breadcrumbs. Add the crumbled cheese and
the watercress. Remove the middle of each onion, leaving
a few layers as an unbroken shell. Chop up the scooped
out pieces of onion and add to the cheese mixture. Press
the mixture into the onion shells. Stand the onions in an
ovenproof dish and dot the top of each with a little butter.
Bake in the oven at gas mark 4, 180°C (350°F) for 40
minutes.

CHEESE AND APPLE BAKE

This is a good dish to serve at lunchtime with a salad.

Serves 4

6 thick slices of bread, crusts removed
butter
1 large eating apple, peeled, cored and grated
175g, 7oz Lancashire cheese, crumbled
3 eggs
450ml, 1¾pts (1½ cups) milk
salt and pepper
4 rashers unsmoked streaky bacon, chopped

Spread butter on the slices of bread. Mix together the grated apple and 150g (6oz) of the cheese. Spread over three slices of the bread and sandwich together with the remaining slices. Cut into halves and arrange over the bottom of an ovenproof dish overlapping if necessary. Beat together the eggs, milk, salt and pepper and pour over the bread. Sprinkle over the rest of the cheese and the chopped bacon. Bake in the oven at gas mark 6, 200°C (400°F) for about 40 minutes until crisp and golden brown.

APPLE AND HAM BAKE

This is similar to the previous recipe and also good for a
light lunch.

Serves 4 - 6

100g, 4oz (1cup) fresh white breadcrumbs
225g, 8oz cooked ham, chopped
1 small onion, peeled and chopped
pinch of ground cloves
½ tsp mustard powder
1 egg, beaten
90ml, 3fl oz (⅓ cup) milk
450g, 1lb eating apples, peeled, cored and sliced
2 tbsp honey
25g, 1oz (2 tbsp) butter

Combine the breadcrumbs, ham, onion, cloves, mustard
powder, beaten egg and milk. Put the ham mixture into a
shallow ovenproof dish and spread out evenly. Arrange the
sliced apples on top, drizzle over the honey and dot with
butter. Bake in the oven at gas mark 5, 190°C (375°F) for
about 40 minutes.

FENNEL AND APPLE GRATIN

2 tbsp olive oil
450g, 1lb fennel, washed and sliced
1 large Bramley apple, peeled, cored and sliced
2 cloves of garlic, peeled and crushed
salt and pepper
75g, 3oz mature Cheddar cheese, grated
450g, 1lb potatoes, preferably Desirée,
peeled and chopped
150ml, 5fl oz (⅔ cup) crème fraîche
120ml, ¼ pt (½ cup) milk
2 tsp grainy mustard
butter

Fry the sliced fennel in the olive oil for a few minutes. Add the apples and garlic and fry for a couple more minutes. Transfer to an ovenproof dish and season with salt and pepper. Sprinkle with the cheese. Meanwhile par-boil the potatoes for a few minutes and then slice thinly and arrange on top of the cheese. Mix together the crème fraîche, milk and mustard and pour over the potatoes. Dot with a little butter and bake in the oven at gas mark 5, 190°C (375°F) for about 1 hour.

APPLE AND LIME ROSTI

Serves 6 - 8

Rosti is a Swiss dish of grated potato and onion which is made into a crisply coated pancake and traditionally cooked in goose fat. Here is a version of a rosti and I've used butter rather than goose fat.

2kg, 4½lb potatoes
350g, 12oz cooking apples, cored and grated
grated rind and juice of 2 limes
1 clove of garlic, skinned and crushed
butter

Cook the potatoes in their skins for 10 minutes. Cool, peel and grate them coarsely. Add lime juice, rind and garlic to the grated apple. Mix the potatoes with the apple. Heat the butter in a large frying pan and add the apple and potato mixture. Press down and cook until the base turns golden brown. Now you can either try and turn the rosti over in the frying pan or stick it under a grill to brown the top. Serve with pork or gammon.

CHESTNUT, APPLE AND PRUNE CASSEROLE

This goes well with gammon, bacon chops or pork.

Serves 4

25g, 1oz (2 tbsp) butter
1 onion, peeled and chopped
*225g, 8oz prunes, soaked in water overnight, drained
and pitted*
225g, 8oz chestnuts, peeled and cooked
1 large cooking apple, peeled, cored and sliced
1 tbsp soft brown sugar
300ml, ½pt (1¼ cups) red wine
1 stick cinnamon
salt and pepper

Melt the butter in a casserole and cook the onion. Stir in the prunes, chestnuts, apples, brown sugar, red wine and cinnamon. Add seasoning. Bring to the boil and then cover and put in the oven at gas mark 4, 180°C (350°F) for 1 hour. Discard the cinnamon stick and serve as a side dish.

PUDDINGS

APPLE PUDDING

This pudding is easy to make and delicious to eat. The contrast of the yellow pudding and purple blackberry sauce is rather effective.

50g, 2oz (¼ cup) butter
50g, 2oz (½ cup) flour
90ml, 3fl oz (⅓ cup) milk
50g, 2oz (⅓ cup) sugar
3 eggs, separated
2 large cooking apples, cored, peeled, and sliced
25g, 1oz (2 tbsp) butter
juice of ½ lemon
1 tbsp caster sugar
sprinkling of cinnamon

Blackberry purée (see page 144)

Melt the butter in a saucepan, stir in the flour and cook for a couple of minutes. Add the milk slowly, stirring all the time until you have a smooth sauce. Beat the sugar with the egg yolks and gradually whisk this mixture into the thickened sauce. Return to the heat and stir until the mixture boils. Spoon into a large bowl and cool. Beat the egg whites and fold them into the cold mixture. Fry the apple slices in a little butter. Add the lemon juice, sugar and cinnamon. Fold into the egg mixture. Pour into an ovenproof dish and stand in a roasting tin of hot water. Bake in the oven at gas mark 4, 180°C (350°F) for 30 minutes. Serve with blackberry purée.

APPLE AND PECAN PUDDING

This is an excellent family pudding to fill everyone up
on a cold winter's day.

150g, 6oz (⅔ cup) butter
75g, 3oz (½ cup) caster sugar
75g, 3oz (¾ cup) light muscovado sugar
3 eggs, beaten
150g, 6oz (1½ cups) self-raising flour
grated rind and juice of 1 lemon
3 eating apples, Cox's or Braeburns, peeled, cored and
sliced

Topping

50g, 2oz (½ cup) pecan nuts, chopped
50g, 2oz (½ cup) light muscovado sugar
50g, 2oz (½ cup) plain flour
¼ tsp cinnamon
50g, 2oz (¼ cup) butter

First make the sponge. Cream together the butter and sugar.
Add the eggs gradually along with the lemon rind. Mix in
the flour and lemon juice. Grease an ovenproof dish and
spread the sponge mixture over the bottom. Lay the slices
of apple over the sponge and sprinkle with a little lemon
juice. To make the topping, mix together the flour,
cinnamon, sugar and pecans and rub in the butter. Spread
over the apples. Bake in the oven at gas mark 5, 190°C
(375°F) for 40 minutes. Serve warm with Greek yoghurt
or crème fraîche.

APPLE AND BLUEBERRY
WALNUT CRISP

The blueberries give the inside of this pudding great colour. The apples melt into the purple fruit.

350g, 12oz blueberries
225g, 8oz cooking apples, peeled, cored and sliced
grated rind and juice of 1 lemon
150g, 6oz (1½ cups) light brown sugar

Topping

150g, 6oz (1½ cups) plain flour
1 tsp baking powder
100g, 4oz (⅔ cup) sugar
50g, 2oz (¼ cup) butter
1 large egg, beaten
a handful of walnuts, chopped
½ tsp cinnamon

Mix the blueberries and apples with the lemon rind and juice and the brown sugar. Spread over a greased ovenproof dish. To make the topping mix together the flour, baking powder and sugar. Rub in the butter, then add the egg and nuts. Spread this mixture over the fruit. Sprinkle the cinnamon over the top. Cook in the oven at gas mark 6, 200°C (400°F) for 30 minutes. The top should be nicely browned. Serve with cream or crème fraîche.

WHEATY APPLE AND
ORANGE PUDDING

Apples and oranges are an unusual combination but go
well together.

3 tbsp wheatgerm soaked for 1 hour in the juice of
2 oranges
300ml, ½pt (1¼ cups) apple purée
4 tbsp chopped walnuts
2 tbsp chopped almonds
1 orange, cut into segments
grated rind of ½ orange
150ml, ¼pt (⅔ cup) Greek yoghurt
2 tbsp soft brown sugar

Put the soaked wheatgerm into a large serving bowl. Mix
the apple purée, walnuts, almonds, orange segments and
rind into the wheat germ. Chill before serving. Spoon over
the yoghurt and sprinkle over the sugar when you are ready
to serve.

APPLE AND GINGER PUDDING

The honey and ginger give this healthy pudding a delicious flavour.

100g, 4oz (1 cup) plain wholemeal flour
50g, 2oz (¼ cup) margarine
25g, 1oz wheatgerm
50g, 2oz (½ cup) soft brown sugar
2 eggs, beaten
4 tbsp milk
3 pieces stem ginger, chopped
1 tbsp juice from stem ginger
2 tbsp thick honey
2 cooking apples, peeled, cored and grated

Rub the margarine into the flour until the mixture resembles breadcrumbs. Add the wheatgerm, sugar and eggs and enough milk to give a dropping consistency. Stir in the pieces of stem ginger and stem ginger juice. Put the honey in a greased ovenproof dish and heat until melted. Spread the grated apple over the base and cover with the pudding mixture. Bake in the oven at gas mark 5, 190°C (375°F) for 30 minutes. Serve hot with Greek yoghurt.

APPLE PAN DOWDY

This is a delicious, dark, fudgy pudding.

1 large Bramley cooking apple, peeled, cored and sliced
4 tbsp black treacle
2 tbsp cold water
4 tbsp soft brown sugar
pinch of ground ginger
pinch of ground cinnamon
pinch of nutmeg
25g, 1oz (2 tbsp) butter
150g, 6oz shortcrust pastry

Lay the sliced apple over the bottom of a greased 20cm (8in) pie dish. Mix together the black treacle and water. Stir the spices into the sugar and add to the treacle. Pour this over the apple. Dot small pieces of butter over the top. Roll the pastry into a circle to fit over the contents of the pie dish and seal it down. Bake in the oven at gas mark 6, 200°C (400°F) for 30 minutes. Take a sharp knife and cut through the pastry marking it roughly into squares over which the filling seeps. Return it to the oven and cook for another 40 minutes until the top is brown and fudge-like. Serve hot with cream or ice-cream.

LINGONBERRY AND APPLE TART

Lingonberries come originally from Sweden - the Arctic cranberry - they are a luscious red. You can buy jars of lingonberry sauce from good supermarkets or delicatessens.

Pastry

225g, 8oz (2 cups) plain flour
100g, 4oz (½ cup) margarine
1 egg yolk
water

4 tbsp lingonberry sauce
225g, 8oz cooking apples, peeled, cored and chopped
grated rind of ½ lemon
3 tbsp lemon juice
25g, 1oz (¼ cup) Brazil nuts, chopped
75g, 3oz (¾ cup) brown sugar
150g, 6oz (1½ cup) raisins
¼ tsp ground cinnamon
¼ tsp ground nutmeg
¼ tsp ground ginger

To make the pastry, rub the margarine into the flour. Bind with the egg yolk and sufficient water to make a firm dough. Knead lightly and then roll out three quarters of the pastry and line a greased 23cm (9in) flan tin. To make the filling cook the apples for 5 minutes in a little water. Mix the apples with the lingonberry sauce and add the lemon rind, lemon juice, Brazil nuts, brown sugar, raisins and spices. Stir well and fill the pastry case with this mixture. Roll out the remaining pastry and cut into strips. Cover the flan with a lattice of strips. Brush with a little egg white if liked and a sprinkling of caster sugar. Bake in the oven at gas mark 4, 180°C (350°F) for 35 minutes.

CARAMEL APPLE TART

Simple ingredients are used here to achieve a lovely toffee top.

Sweet pastry

150g, 6oz (1½ cups) plain flour
75g, 3oz (⅓ cup) butter
40g, 1½oz (¼ cup) icing sugar
1 egg yolk
1 tbsp water

450g, 1lb eating apples, peeled, cored and sliced
100g, 4oz (⅔ cup) caster sugar
25g, 1oz (2 tbsp) butter
1 tbsp water

For the pastry rub the butter into the flour and icing sugar. Bind together with the egg yolk and water and knead lightly. Chill for 30 minutes. Melt the sugar with 15g, ½oz (1 tbsp) of the butter and the water in a saucepan until it turns a golden colour. Pour it quickly over a greased 20cm (8in) flan dish and spread over the surface of the dish. Arrange the apple slices over the toffee. Dot them with the rest of the butter and sprinkle on a little more sugar. Roll out the pastry and cover the apples with it. Bake in the oven at gas mark 6, 200°C (400°F) for 30 minutes. Turn the tart out so that the toffee is on top. Serve hot with cream.

APPLE AND LEMON TARTLETS

These are delicious with cream.

*shortcrust pastry made with 150g, 6oz (1½ cups) plain
flour and 75g, 3oz (⅓ cup) margarine*

*450g, 1lb cooking apples, peeled, cored and thinly sliced
3 eggs
150ml ¼pt (⅔ cup) single cream
75g, 3oz (½ cup) caster sugar
grated rind and juice of 1 lemon*

Roll out the pastry and divide into four circles to fit into a greased tartlet tin. Bake blind in the oven at gas mark 4, 180°C (350°F) for 15 minutes. Beat the eggs, cream and sugar together. Add the grated lemon rind and juice and whisk until smooth. Arrange the apple slices in the tartlets and cover with the egg and lemon mixture. Return to the oven and bake for about 25 minutes. Serve with cream or Greek yoghurt.

APPLE AND MASCARPONE
STREUSEL PIE

This sort of pie has a pastry base, a filling and a crumble topping.

shortcrust pastry made with 150g, 6oz (1½ cups) plain flour and 75g, 3oz (⅓ cup) margarine

Filling

100g, 4oz (½ cup) mascarpone
50g, 2oz (½ cup) brown sugar
2 eggs
50g, 2oz (½ cup) plain flour
½ tsp vanilla essence
225g, 8oz apples, peeled, cored and sliced

Topping

50g, 2oz (½ cup) self-raising flour
50g, 2oz (⅓ cup) demerara sugar
100g, 4oz (1 cup) pecan nuts
75g, 3oz (⅓ cup) butter

Line a deep, greased 20cm (8in) pie dish with the pastry. Mix together the mascarpone, brown sugar, eggs, flour and vanilla essence. Fill the pie dish with slices of apple. Pour over the mascarpone mixture. Now cook in the oven at gas mark 4, 180°C (350°F) for 30 minutes. To make the topping mix together all the ingredients. Add the topping to the pie and return to the oven for 15 minutes.

APPLE AND DAMSON PIE

100g, 4oz (1 cup) plain flour
75g, 3oz (⅓ cup) butter
1 egg yolk
squeeze of lemon juice
cold water
milk
caster sugar

Filling

650g, 1½lb cooking apples, peeled, cored and sliced
225g, 8oz damsons
25g, 1oz (2 tbsp) butter
50g, 2oz (⅓ cup) granulated sugar
2 strips lemon rind
2 cloves

Rub the butter into the flour. Mix the egg yolk with a squeeze of lemon juice and a little water and mix into the flour and butter to make a smooth dough. Wrap in cling film and chill for 30 minutes. Meanwhile make the filling. Melt the butter in a saucepan and add the sugar, lemon rind, cloves and apples. Toss over the heat until the apples are beginning to soften. Mix the apples with the damsons and tip into a large pie dish. Roll out the pastry into a circle slightly larger than the pie dish. Cover the pie with the pastry and seal down the pastry round the rim with a little water. Make a hole in the centre of the pie. Brush with a little milk and dust with caster sugar. Bake in the oven at gas mark 5, 190°C (375°F) for 30 minutes.

APRICOT AND APPLE ROLL

225g, 8oz packet puff pastry
15g, ½oz (1 tbsp) butter, melted
1 cooking apple, peeled, cored and grated
juice of ½ lemon
50g, 2oz (⅓ cup) caster sugar
¼ tsp cinnamon
50g, 2oz dried apricots, soaked overnight
1 egg, beaten

Roll out the pastry into a rectangle and brush with melted butter. Mix the apple, lemon juice, sugar and cinnamon together. Drain the apricots, make sure the stones are removed and chop them. Add to the apple mixture. Spread the mixture over the pastry, leaving a gap of 1cm (½in) around the edges. Roll up the pastry to form a Swiss roll shape. Seal the join with a little water. Place on a baking sheet, brush with the beaten egg, sprinkle with a little extra caster sugar and cinnamon. Bake in the oven at gas mark 6, 200°C (400°F) for about 30 minutes. Remove from the oven, leave to cool slightly and then cut into slices.

MAPLE SYRUP AND APPLE
UPSIDE DOWN SPONGE

120ml, 4fl oz (½ cup) maple syrup
225g, 8oz cooking apples, peeled, cored and thinly sliced
100g, 4oz (⅔ cup) sugar
100g, 4oz (½ cup) butter
2 eggs
100g, 4oz (1 cup) self-raising flour

Pour the maple syrup in the bottom of a pie dish. Cover with slices of apple. Make the sponge by combining the butter, sugar, eggs and flour. Mix everything together with an electric whisk. Spread the sponge mixture over the apples and bake in the oven at gas mark 4, 180°C (350°F) for 40 minutes. Turn out of the tin so that the apples, glazed with the maple syrup, are on the top.

APPLE AND RASPBERRY SPONGE

450g, 1lb Cox's apples, peeled, cored and chopped
450g, 1lb raspberries
75g, 3oz (½ cup) demerara sugar
1 tbsp lemon juice
25g, 1oz (2 tbsp) butter

Sponge

100g, 4oz (½ cup) margarine
100g, 4oz (⅔ cup) caster sugar
100g, 4oz (1 cup) self-raising flour
2 eggs, beaten

Melt the butter in a large saucepan and add the chopped apples, raspberries, lemon juice and sugar. Gently heat to dissolve the sugar and cook for 5 minutes. Tip the whole mixture into an ovenproof dish. To make the sponge, combine all the ingredients in a food processor or cream together the margarine and sugar and add the eggs gradually with the flour. Spread the sponge mixture over the apples and raspberries. Cook in the oven at gas mark 4, 180°C (350°F) for 30 minutes.

CARAMELISED APPLE SPONGE

This would be suitable for a winter supper party.

50g, 2oz (¼ cup) butter
3 tbsp demerara sugar
2 tbsp cider vinegar
450g, 1lb eating apples, peeled, cored and chopped

Sponge

100g, 4oz (½ cup) butter
100g, 4oz (⅔ cup) caster sugar
2 eggs
100g, 4oz (1 cup) self-raising flour

First put the butter and sugar in a saucepan and heat gently.
When the butter has melted, turn up the heat and stirring
with a wooden spoon let the mixture bubble and darken.
Add the vinegar (be careful, the mixture will splutter) and
drop in the sliced apples. Cook for about 15 minutes turning
the apples every so often. Try not to allow them to break
up. Transfer to a dish and leave to cool. For the sponge,
combine all four ingredients in a food processor or cream
the butter and sugar together and add the eggs gradually
with the flour. Spread half the sponge mixture over the
base of a greased pie dish, pour the apples over this and
cover with the rest of the sponge mixture. Bake in the oven
at gas mark 4, 180°C (350°F) for 30 minutes. Stick a skewer
in to make sure the sponge is cooked in the middle. If still
gooey, return to the oven for another 10 or 15 minutes.

APPLE AND PINE NUTS WITH
POLENTA CRUMBLE

Polenta is a maize flour which can be bought in large
supermarkets or delicatessens.

450g, 1lb eating apples, peeled, cored and sliced
25g, 1oz (2 tbsp) butter
50g, 2oz (½ cup) pine nuts
1 tsp cinnamon
50g, 2oz (½ cup) soft light brown sugar
grated rind and juice of ½ lemon

Crumble topping

75g, 3oz (¾ cup) polenta
75g, 3oz (¾ cup) plain flour
75g, 3oz (⅓ cup) butter
50g, 2oz (⅓ cup) golden caster sugar

Fry the apple slices in the butter in a frying pan. After a
few minutes add the pine nuts and stir them around for a
minute. Then add the cinnamon, sugar, lemon rind and juice
and cook until the juices evaporate. Put the apples in the
base of a pie tin. To make the topping, rub the butter into
the polenta and flour and mix in the caster sugar. Spread
over the apple mixture. Bake in the oven at gas mark 4,
180°C (350°F) for 30 minutes.

APPLE SOUFFLÉ OMELETTE

This a quick, easy pudding and is really yummy.

Filling

1 Cox's apple, peeled, cored and sliced
25g, 1oz (2 tbsp) butter
2 tbsp light brown sugar
3 tbsp single cream

3 large eggs, separated
2 tbsp single cream
1 tbsp caster sugar
15g, ½oz (1 tbsp) butter

For the filling, gently fry the slices of apple in the butter and sugar until tender. Stir in the cream and keep warm. To make the omelette, beat the egg yolks with the cream and sugar. Whisk the egg whites and fold them in. Melt the butter in a frying pan and pour in the egg mixture. Fry the omelette so that it browns underneath. Then place under a grill to brown the top. Add the apple filling and fold over. Dust with icing sugar and serve at once.

APPLE CRUNCH WITH LEMON CREAM

300ml, ½pt (1¼ cups) sweetened apple purée
50g, 2oz (¼ cup) butter
100g, 4oz (1 cup) brown breadcrumbs
50g, 2oz (½ cup) brown sugar
1 tsp cinnamon
150ml, ¼pt (⅔ cup) thick cream
2 tbsp lemon curd

To make the apple purée, cook 450g, 1lb cooking apples with a little water and sugar to taste until soft. Beat to a purée. Melt the butter in a frying pan and add the breadcrumbs, sugar and cinnamon. Mix well and fry until crisp and brown. Allow to cool. Mix the cream and lemon curd together. Make layers in a serving bowl of apple purée, breadcrumb mixture and the lemon cream, ending with a layer of breadcrumbs.

BAKED APPLES

6 Bramley cooking apples, cored
50g, 2oz (¼ cup) butter
450g, 1lb dried figs, chopped
6 tbsp ground almonds
3 tbsp sherry

Keep the skin on the apples but cut a slit around the middle of each apple. This prevents the baked apples from bursting when in the oven. Melt half the butter and add the figs, almonds and the sherry. Cook for 5 minutes. Fill the apples with this mixture and top each one with a little of the remaining butter. Cook on a greased baking tray in the oven at gas mark 4, 180°C (350°F) for 30 minutes.

APPLE AND ORANGE BRISTOL

75g, 3oz (½ cup) granulated sugar
300ml, ½pt (1¼ cups) water
4 Cox's apples, peeled, cored and sliced
½ tsp vanilla essence
3 oranges, peeled and pith removed

Caramel

100g, 4oz (⅔ cup) sugar
150ml, ¼pt (⅔ cup) water

Dissolve the sugar gently in the water, then boil rapidly for 1 minute. Add the apples and vanilla essence and simmer for 15 minutes. Remove from the heat and cool. Cut some of the peel from one of the oranges into strips and boil in a little water for 5 minutes. Drain and set aside. Slice the oranges into rounds. To make the caramel, dissolve the sugar in the water and boil until it turns brown. Pour onto a greased baking sheet and leave to set, before breaking into pieces. Arrange the apples and oranges in a serving bowl with the syrup from the apples. Sprinkle the orange rind strips over the top along with the pieces of caramel. Chill before serving.

BAKED APPLE CHEESECAKE

350g, 12oz cooking apples, peeled, cored and sliced
50g, 2oz (⅓ cup) granulated sugar
100g, 4oz (½ cup) butter
100g, 4oz (1 cup) light brown sugar
450g, 1lb cottage cheese
2 eggs, separated
50g, 2oz (½ cup) semolina

Cook the apples with a spoonful of water and the granulated sugar until tender but don't let them break up. Cream together the butter and sugar. Beat in the cheese and egg yolks. Gradually fold in the semolina and the sliced apple. Whisk the egg whites until stiff and fold them into the apple mixture. Spoon the mixture into a greased 20cm (8in) pie dish and bake in the oven at gas mark 5, 190°C (375°F) for 45 minutes. Leave to cool in the tin. Dust with icing sugar before serving.

APPLES GRATINÉES

A slightly different apple meringue pudding.

4 large Bramley apples, peeled, cored and sliced
a little butter
2 tbsp apricot jam
grated rind and juice of 1 lemon
100g, 4oz (1 cup) brown sugar
3 eating apples, peeled, cored and quartered
100g, 4oz (⅔ cup) granulated sugar
water

Meringue

2 egg whites
100g, 4oz (⅔ cup) caster sugar
25g, 1oz (¼ cup) ground almonds
icing sugar

Cook the sliced Bramley apples with the jam, lemon rind, juice and brown sugar until soft. Beat to a purée. Cool slightly and spread over the base of a round pie dish. Poach the eating apples in a syrup made from the granulated sugar and water. Do not allow them to break up. Drain and arrange on top of the apple purée. Whip the whites until stiff and gradually beat in the sugar. Fold in the ground almonds. Spread the meringue mixture over the apple, sprinkle with a little icing sugar and cook in a slow oven at gas mark 3, 160°C (325°F) for 30 minutes.

APPLE PAPANAS

Papana is a type of pancake which originated in Romania. Papanas are served with soured cream and chives in Romania but in this recipe they go well with apple purée.

225g, 8oz fromage frais
2 egg yolks
100g, 4oz (1 cup) plain flour
1 egg white, beaten
90ml, 3fl oz (⅓ cup) sunflower oil
450g, 1lb Bramley apples, peeled, cored and sliced
2 tbsp lemon juice
75g, 3oz (¾ cup) light brown sugar
1 small tub of crème fraîche

Beat the egg yolks into the fromage frais in a large bowl. Add the flour gradually mixing it in carefully. Fold in the beaten egg white. Heat the oil in a large frying pan and fry tablespoons of the mixture. When browned, remove and place on kitchen paper. Cook the apples, with the sugar and lemon juice, in a covered saucepan for 20 minutes until light and fluffy. Serve the pancakes with the crème fraîche and stewed apples.

SPICY APPLE FOOL

450g, 1lb cooking apples, peeled, cored and sliced
1 tsp mixed spice
1 clove
grated rind of ½ lemon
50g, 2oz (⅓ cup) granulated sugar
150ml, ¼pt (⅔ cup) ready made custard
150ml, ¼pt (⅔ cup) double cream, whipped

Cook the apple slices over a gentle heat with the mixed spice, clove, lemon rind and sugar and a little water. Remove the clove and beat to a purée. Fold in the custard and whipped cream.

APPLE FRITTERS WITH GINGER BEER

100g, 4oz (1 cup) plain flour
1 egg, separated
1 tbsp sunflower oil
150ml, ¼pt (⅔ cup) ginger beer
50g, 2oz (⅓ cup) caster sugar
3 cooking apples, peeled, cored and cut into thick rings

Sift the flour, add the egg yolk and the tablespoon of oil and gradually beat in the ginger beer. Stir in the caster sugar. Beat the egg white and fold it in. Heat some oil in a frying pan and dip each apple ring in the batter before frying them on both sides until brown and crisp. Serve hot sprinkled with sugar.

TEA-TIME TREATS

APPLE MUFFINS

225g, 8oz (2 cups) plain flour
3 tsp baking powder
50g, 2oz (⅓ cup) caster sugar
2 eggs, beaten
150ml, ¼pt (⅔ cup) milk
50g, 2oz (¼ cup) butter, melted
225g, 8oz eating apples, Cox's or Royal Gala, peeled,
cored and chopped

Sift the flour, baking powder and sugar into a bowl. Beat the eggs with the milk and mix in the butter. Stir this liquid into the flour. Fold in the apples and spoon into greased muffin tins so that each one is about a third full. Bake in the oven at gas mark 7, 220°C (450°F) for 15 minutes. Serve hot with jam or honey, if liked.

APPLE AND PECAN LOAF

This is an unusual pastry and sponge loaf topped
with apples.

225g, 8oz (2 cups) plain flour
225g, 8oz (1 cup) margarine
3 eggs, beaten
100g, 4oz (⅔ cup) light brown sugar
100g, 4oz (1 cup) self-raising flour
¼ tsp ground cinnamon
150g, 6oz (1½ cups) pecans
2 eating apples, Cox's or Discovery, peeled, cored and
sliced
1 tbsp demerara sugar

Rub together the plain flour and 100g, 4oz *(½ cup)* of the
margarine. Knead to a dough with one of the eggs and a
little water if needed. Chill. Roll out the pastry and use to
line a greased 1.4litre, 2pt loaf tin. Chill again. Cream the
remaining margarine with the sugar. Gradually beat in the
remaining eggs. Fold in the self-raising flour, cinnamon
and pecans. Spoon the sponge over the pastry. Arrange the
apple slices on top. Sprinkle demerara sugar over the apples.
Bake at gas mark 5, 190°C (375°F) for about 1 hour. Cool,
turn out and cut into slices.

APPLE GINGERBREAD

This is delicious and a good way of filling up the
whole family.

450g, 1lb eating apples, peeled, cored and chopped
25g, 1oz (2 tbsp) butter
225g, 8oz (2 cups) plain flour
2 tsp baking powder
3 tsp ground ginger
50g, 2oz (¼ cup) margarine
100g, 4oz (¾ cup) medium oatmeal
75g, 3oz (½ cup) caster sugar
100g, 4oz golden syrup
100g, 4oz black treacle
1 egg, beaten
2 tbsp milk

Cook the apples with the butter in a saucepan until soft.
Beat to a purée. Meanwhile sift the flour with the baking
powder and ginger in a large bowl. Rub in the margarine.
Stir in the oatmeal and sugar. Warm the syrup and black
treacle and then stir into the dry ingredients together with
the apple purée, egg and milk. Stir until everything is mixed
well together. Turn into a 1.7l, 3pt loaf tin and bake in the
oven at gas mark 4, 180°C (350°F) for about 1½ hours,
covering with foil if the top gets too brown. Turn out and
cool. This gingerbread is best stored for two days before
eating.

APPLE AND PEAR CAKE

This is a solid but moist cake which can be eaten in
one's fingers.

1 cooking apple, peeled, cored and chopped
1 pear, cored, peeled and chopped
juice of ½ lemon
225g, 8oz (2 cups) plain wholemeal flour
1 tsp ground nutmeg
1 tsp cinnamon
100g, 4oz (½ cup) butter
150g, 6oz (1 cup) demerara sugar
2 large eggs, beaten

Toss the apple and pear pieces in the lemon juice. Sift the
flour with the spices and add to the apple and pear. Cream
the butter and sugar together. Mix in the eggs a little at a
time. Fold in the apple and pear mixture. Grease a 20cm
(8in) cake tin and spoon in the cake mixture. Bake in the
oven at gas mark 3, 160°C (325°F) for 1 hour. Take out
and cool before serving.

PRESERVES

APPLE AND LOGANBERRY SAUCE

Makes 3 - 4 jars

450g, 1lb loganberries
450g, 1lb apples, peeled, cored and chopped
900g, 2lb (6 cups) granulated sugar
2 handfuls of mint leaves

Put the loganberries in a large saucepan and heat gently until the juices begin to run. Add the apples and cook until the apples are soft. Add the sugar and stir to dissolve it. Next add the mint and boil for 10 minutes. Allow to cool for 30 minutes. Give the sauce a stir before pouring into jars.

APPLE AND LEMON MARMALADE

Makes 5 jars

juice, peel and pips of 3 lemons
450g, 1lb cooking apples, peeled and cored (reserve peel and cores)
1.8l, 3pt water
900g, 2lb (2 cups) sugar
450g, 1lb (1½ cups) honey

Put the lemon juice and the lemon peel, cut into shreds, into a large saucepan. Add the apples. Tie the apple peel, cores and lemon pips into a piece of muslin and add to the pan. Pour in the water and bring to the boil. Simmer for 1½ hours. Remove the muslin. Add the sugar and honey and stir over a low heat until dissolved. Boil rapidly until setting point is reached. Remove any scum. Allow to cool slightly and then pour into warm jars.

APPLE AND ELDERBERRY CHUTNEY

Makes 3 - 4 jars

450g, 1lb elderberries, stalks removed
450g, 1lb onions, peeled and chopped
450g, 1lb cooking apples, peeled, cored and sliced
50g, 2oz (½ cup) raisins
50g, 2oz (½ cup) sultanas
1 tsp mixed spice
1 tsp ginger
1 tsp salt
¼ tsp cayenne pepper
300ml, ½pt (1¼ cups) malt vinegar
350g, 12oz (2 cups) sugar

Put the elderberries, onions and apples together in a large saucepan. Add raisins, sultanas, spices, salt, cayenne pepper and half the vinegar. Bring to the boil and simmer until the fruits are tender. Add the sugar and rest of the vinegar. Stir over a low heat for 15 minutes. Pour into jars and seal.

APPLE AND MINT CHUTNEY

Makes 3 jars

1.3kg, 3lb cooking apples, peeled, cored and chopped
900ml, 1½pt (3¾ cups) spiced vinegar
½ tsp coriander
1 tsp black pepper
2 dried red chillies
450g, 1lb (2⅔ cup) demerara sugar
2 tsp salt
2 tbsp chopped mint

Put the apples in a saucepan with the vinegar and bring slowly to the boil. Place the spices, pepper and chillies in some muslin and tie up. Add to the pan with the sugar and salt. Simmer until thick. Remove the muslin and stir in the mint. Pour into jars and seal.

APPLE, SLOE AND ROSEHIP JELLY

Makes 3 - 4 jars

1kg, 2.2lb cooking apples, chopped
200g, 7oz sloes
200g, 7oz rosehips
sugar
juice of 1 lemon

Chop up the apples roughly. Prick the sloes with a pin all over. Top and tail the rosehips. Put all the fruit in a large saucepan with 2 litres, 3½ pints of water. Simmer gently for about 1 hour. Pour the fruit into a jelly or muslin bag and allow to drip through overnight. Measure the juice. For every 500ml, 16 fl oz add 350g, 12oz of sugar. Put in a preserving pan with the lemon juice and dissolve the sugar over a gentle heat. Raise the heat and boil hard until setting point is reached. Pour into warm jars and seal.

APPLES AND BLACKBERRIES

PUDDINGS

Apples and blackberries go so well together that I have devoted a special section to them. Apple and blackberry purée is delicious and is used in several of the following recipes.

APPLE AND BLACKBERRY PURÉE

450g, 1lb cooking apples, peeled, cored and sliced
225g, 8oz blackberries
100g, 4oz (⅔ cup) sugar

Combine the apples, blackberries and sugar in a saucepan and cover. Cook gently for about 20 minutes. Purée in a food processor and sieve the mixture to remove the blackberry pips.

APPLE AND BLACKBERRY PIE

shortcrust pastry made with 225g, 8oz (2 cups) plain flour and 100g, 4oz (½ cup) margarine

225g, 8oz cooking apples, peeled, cored and sliced
100g, 4oz blackberries
100g, 4oz (⅔ cup) granulated sugar
1 tbsp water
1 tbsp cornflour

Put the apples, blackberries, sugar and water in a saucepan and simmer gently for about 20 minutes. Blend the cornflour with a little cold water and stir into the fruit. Cook for a couple of minutes until the mixture is thick. Roll out the pastry into two rounds, one slightly bigger than the other. Use the smaller half to line the base of a greased 20cm (8in) pie dish. Pour the fruit onto the pastry. Cover with the pastry lid and seal round the edges using a little cold water. Make a little slit in the top of the pie for the steam to escape. Brush with a little milk and a sprinkling of caster sugar. Bake in the oven at gas mark 6, 200°C (400°F) for about 40 minutes.

APPLE AND BLACKBERRY TART

*shortcrust pastry made with 150g, 6oz (1½ cups) plain
flour and 75g, 3oz (⅓ cup) margarine*

*100g, 4oz blackberries
75g, 3oz (½ cup) sugar
3 tsp cornflour
1 large cooking apple, peeled, cored and grated
1 egg*

Roll out the pastry and place in a greased 20cm (8in) flan
dish. Bake blind in the oven at gas mark 5, 190°C (375°F)
for 15 minutes. Meanwhile cook the blackberries with the
sugar in a saucepan with a tightly fitting lid until the juices
begin to run and the blackberries are tender. Sieve them to
remove the pips. Mix the cornflour with a little water to a
smooth paste. Then gradually add to the blackberry purée
over a gentle heat stirring all the time until the purée has
thickened. Grate the apple and mix with the beaten egg.
Spread this over the pastry case and then spread the blackberry mixture evenly over the top of the apple. Bake in the
oven at gas mark 4, 180°C (350°F) for 30 minutes.

APPLE AND BLACKBERRY TREACLE TART

shortcrust pastry made with 150g, 6oz (1½ cups) plain flour and 75g, 3oz (⅓ cup) margarine

2 eggs
150ml, ¼pt (⅔ cup) whipping cream
1 cooking apple, peeled, cored and grated
2 tbsp blackberry purée
6 tbsp golden syrup
50g, 2oz (½ cup) brown breadcrumbs
grated rind and juice of ½ lemon

Roll out the pastry and use to line a greased 20cm (8in) flan dish. Beat the eggs and whisk in the cream. Add the grated apple, blackberry purée, golden syrup, breadcrumbs, lemon rind and juice. Mix well together. Pour over the pastry case and bake in the oven at gas mark 4, 180°C (350°F) for 25 minutes.

APPLE AND BLACKBERRY AMBER

shortcrust pastry made with 150g, 6oz (1½ cups) plain
flour and 75g, 3oz (⅓ cup) margarine

450g, 1lb cooking apples, peeled, cored and sliced
100g, 4oz blackberries
juice of 1 lemon
100g, 4oz (1 cup) brown sugar
2 eggs, separated
100g, 4oz (⅔ cup) caster sugar

Roll out the pastry and use to line a greased 20cm (8in) flan dish. Bake blind in the oven at gas mark 5, 190°C (375°F) for 15 minutes. Cook the apples and blackberries with the lemon and brown sugar over a gentle heat for 15 minutes. Sieve the apple and blackberry mixture and when slightly cooled mix in the egg yolks. Spread over the pastry base. Whisk the egg whites until stiff and whisk in the sugar bit by bit until the meringue is thick and glossy. Spread over the blackberry and apple. Bake in the oven at gas mark 3, 160°C (325°F) for a further 40 minutes, by which time the meringue will be golden and crisp on top but soft inside. Serve with cream.

CORIANDER, APPLE AND
BLACKBERRY CRUMBLE

650g, 1½lb cooking apples, peeled, cored and sliced
225g, 8oz blackberries
2 tbsp soft brown sugar
1 tsp cinnamon

Crumble topping

100g, 4oz (1 cup) flour
100g, 4oz (⅔ cup) sugar
100g, 4oz (½ cup) butter
2 tsp ground coriander

Grease a baking dish with butter and put the apples and blackberries in the dish. Sprinkle with brown sugar and cinnamon. To make the crumble, rub the butter into the flour and sugar until it resembles breadcrumbs. Mix in the coriander and sprinkle the crumble over the apples and blackberries. Cook in the oven at gas mark 4, 180°C (350°F) for 45 minutes.

APPLE AND BLACKBERRY STRUDEL

225g, 8oz packet puff pastry

225g, 8oz cooking apples, peeled, cored and sliced
2 tbsp lemon juice
50g, 2oz (⅓ cup) demerara sugar
50g, 2oz (½ cup) breadcrumbs
50g, 2oz (½ cup) ground almonds
100g, 4oz blackberries, washed
25g, 1oz (¼ cup) flaked almonds
2 tbsp caster sugar

Mix the apples with the lemon juice, sugar, breadcrumbs, ground almonds and blackberries. Roll out the pastry on a floured surface into a rectangle. Spoon the apple mixture into the middle of the rectangle. Brush the pastry with a little milk and fold the edges over the apple to enclose it completely. Place on a greased baking tray, seam side down, brush with milk, and sprinkle with sugar and the flaked almonds. Cook in the oven at gas mark 5, 190°C (375°F) for 30 minutes. Cut into slices before serving.

APPLE AND BLACKBERRY CHARLOTTE

450g, 1lb cooking apples, peeled, cored and sliced
450g, 1lb blackberries
rind and juice of ½ lemon
¼ tsp cinnamon
225g, 8oz (1⅓ cups) sugar
2 tbsp breadcrumbs
6 slices of bread, with crusts removed
50g, 2oz (¼ cup) butter, melted

Cook the apples and blackberries with the lemon rind, juice and cinnamon for 10 minutes. Add the sugar and breadcrumbs. Grease a Charlotte mould or 20cm (8in) round cake tin. Dip the slices of bread in the melted butter and lay them on the bottom and sides of the tin, keeping enough slices for the top. Spoon the stewed apple and black-berry into the tin and cover with the remaining bread. Bake in the oven at gas mark 5, 190°C (375°F) for 1 hour. Turn out and serve with cream or crème fraîche.

APPLE AND BLACKBERRY FUDGE PUDDING

Sponge base

125g, 5oz (1¼ cups) flour
1 tsp baking powder
2 tbsp caster sugar
50g, 2oz (¼ cup) butter
1 large egg
½ tsp vanilla essence
90ml, 3fl oz (⅓ cup) milk

Topping

450g, 1lb cooking apples, peeled, cored and sliced
100g, 4oz blackberries
50g, 2oz (¼ cup) butter
150g, 6oz (1½ cups) dark brown sugar
1 tsp cinnamon

To make the sponge, mix together the flour, baking powder and sugar. Rub in the butter with your fingertips, as though you are making pastry, until the mixture is like breadcrumbs. Whisk the egg and vanilla essence together and add the milk. Stir into the flour and butter mixture and transfer the batter to a buttered, rectangular, ovenproof dish measuring about 25 x 20cm (10 by 8in). Arrange the apple slices with the blackberries on top of the sponge mixture. Lastly, melt the butter, stir in the brown sugar and cinnamon and pour over the fruit. Bake in the oven at gas mark 6, 200°C (400°F) for 25 minutes.

APPLE AND BLACKBERRY
MERINGUE CAKE

100g, 4oz (½ cup) margarine
100g, 4oz (⅔ cup) sugar
2 eggs
100g, 4oz (1 cup) self-raising flour
60ml, 2fl oz (¼ cup) milk
1 tsp vanilla essence

Meringue

2 egg whites
100g, 4oz (⅔ cup) caster sugar

Filling

450g, 1lb cooking apples, peeled, cored and sliced
100g, 4oz blackberries
25g, 1oz (¼ cup) sugar

Cream the margarine and sugar together. Beat in the eggs and mix in the flour, milk and vanilla essence. Divide this sponge mixture between two greased 18cm (7in) cake tins. To make the meringue, whisk the egg whites and gradually whisk in the caster sugar. Pour half over each sponge mixture. Bake in the oven at gas mark 4, 180°C (350°F) for 45 minutes. Meanwhile cook the apples and blackberries gently with the sugar, but with no water, for 15 minutes. Allow to cool. Sandwich the cakes together with a layer of whipped cream and a layer of the stewed apple and blackberry.

AUTUMN FRUIT DUMPLINGS

*shortcrust pastry made with 225g, 8oz (2 cups) plain
flour and 100g, 4oz (½ cup) margarine*

*4 large Bramley cooking apples, peeled and cored
225g, 8oz blackberries
grated rind of 1 orange
4 tbsp soft light brown sugar
½ tsp ground cinnamon*

Cut the shortcrust pastry into quarters and roll into four
circles. Mix the blackberries with the orange rind, sugar
and cinnamon. Put some of this mixture into the middle of
each apple and place one apple on each pastry circle. Fold
the pastry around each apple and dampen the edges with
water or milk so that you can seal the edges. Place the
dumplings on a greased baking sheet. Brush with a little
milk and bake in the oven at gas mark 6, 200°C (400°F)
for 30 minutes.

AUTUMN PUDDING WITH APPLES, BLACKBERRIES AND PLUMS

This is delicious and a change from the more usual summer pudding.

225g, 8oz cooking apples, peeled, cored and sliced
225g, 8oz blackberries
225g, 8oz plums, halved and de-stoned
150g, 6oz (1 cup) granulated sugar
10 slices of white bread

Cook the apples, plums and blackberries together with the sugar and 4 tablespoons of water until tender. Line the bottom and sides of a 1.1litre, 2pt pudding basin with the bread. Reserve a little of the juice from the fruit. Pour the stewed fruit into the basin and top with a slice of bread to make a lid. Put a plate on top of the basin and weight it down. Chill the pudding overnight. Turn out onto a serving dish. Pour the reserved juice over the top to conceal any white bits of bread.

APPLE AND BLACKBERRY MOUSSE

450g, 1lb cooking apples, peeled, cored and sliced
450g, 1lb blackberries
150ml, ¼pt (⅔ cup) water
100g, 4oz (⅔ cup) caster sugar
juice of 1 lemon
15g, ½oz gelatine or vege-gel
2 egg whites

Cook the apples and blackberries in the water with 75g, 3oz (½ cup) of the sugar. Cover and simmer for 15 minutes. Soak the gelatine in the lemon juice. Add the gelatine to the cooked fruit and stir. Then rub the fruit through a sieve. Allow the fruit purée to cool and start to set. Whisk the egg whites, add the remaining sugar and whisk again. Fold into the fruit purée and transfer to a serving bowl. Chill until set.

APPLE AND BLACKBERRY ICE CREAM

This is an easy ice cream to make and you don't need an
ice cream maker.

3 eggs, separated
300ml, ½pt (1¼ cups) apple and blackberry purée (see
page 130)
125g, 5oz (¾ cup) caster sugar
300ml, ½pt (1¼ cups) double cream

Beat the egg yolks with the sugar until thick and creamy.
Fold in the apple and blackberry purée. Whip the cream
and fold that in too. Lastly whisk the egg whites until stiff.
Fold them into the apple and blackberry mixture. Pour into
a freezer container and freeze until firm.

BLACKBERRIES

MAINLY PUDDINGS

BLACKBERRY PURÉE

Several of the following recipes require blackberry purée and this is how you make it.

Cook your blackberries with sugar to taste and a dash of lemon juice very gently in a saucepan with a tight fitting lid until the juices begin to run. Continue to cook gently until the blackberries are tender. Rub the blackberries through a sieve and discard the pips.

BLACKBERRY JELLY

Gently heat blackberries in a large saucepan with enough water to barely cover them. When the blackberries are soft, pour into muslin and suspend over a bowl so that the blackberry juice runs out of the muslin. Leave overnight and squeeze out any remaining juice in the morning. Use 450g, 1lb of sugar for every 600ml, 1 pt of blackberry juice that you have. Stir the sugar into the juice in a preserving pan or large saucepan and bring to a rolling boil. Boil until the jam is set. You can test for a set by dropping a small amount of the liquid onto a plate and seeing if it has become jelly-like.

BLACKBERRY TART

*shortcrust pastry made with 150g, 6oz (1½ cups) plain
flour and 75g, 3oz (⅓ cup) margarine*

*450g, 1lb blackberries
100g, 4oz (1 cup) brown sugar
300ml, ½pt (1¼ cups) double cream
2 egg yolks*

Roll out the pastry and line a greased 23cm (9in) flan dish
with it. Prick the bottom and bake blind in the oven at gas
mark 5, 190°C (375°F)for about 15 minutes. Fill the pastry
case with the blackberries and brown sugar. Beat the cream
and egg yolks together and pour over the blackberries. Bake
in the oven at gas mark 3, 160°C (325°F) for 30 minutes or
until set.

BLACKBERRY AND PORT STREUSEL

*450g,1lb blackberries
4 tbsp port
50g, 2oz (⅓ cup) caster sugar
100g, 4oz (1 cup) plain flour
75g, 3oz (⅓ cup) butter
75g, 3oz (¾ cup) soft brown sugar*

Put the blackberries into a greased ovenproof dish and
sprinkle the port and the sugar over them. Rub the butter
into the flour until it resembles breadcrumbs. Stir in the
brown sugar. Spread this mixture over the blackberries.
Cook in the oven at gas mark 5, 190°C (375°F) for 30
minutes.

QUEEN OF PUDDINGS

A traditional pudding which takes a little time to prepare but the family will love it.

600ml, 1pt (2½ cups) milk
rind of 1 lemon
25g, 1oz (2 tbsp) butter
150g, 6oz (1 cup) caster sugar
75g, 3oz (¾ cup) fresh white breadcrumbs
3 eggs, separated
4 tbsp blackberry jelly

Heat the milk in a saucepan with the pared lemon rind until the milk is just starting to form a skin. Remove from the heat and stir in the butter and 50g, 2oz (⅓ cup) of the sugar. Take out the lemon rind and stir until the sugar and butter are melted. Stir in the breadcrumbs and set aside for 30 minutes. Once it has rested beat the egg yolks into the breadcrumb mixture and pour into a buttered ovenproof dish. Put in a roasting tin half filled with water and bake in the oven at gas mark 3, 160°C (325°F) for 45 minutes. Remove from the oven. Spread the blackberry jelly over the surface. Whisk the egg whites and gradually add the remaining sugar. When the meringue is very stiff, spoon it over the jelly and bake in the oven for another 30 minutes until the meringue is golden. Serve with cream.

BLACKBERRY AND SYRUP SPONGE

450g, 1lb blackberries
4 tbsp golden syrup
150g, 6oz (¾ cup) butter
150g, 6oz (1 cup) caster sugar
3 eggs, beaten
150g, 6oz (1½ cup) self-raising flour
½ tsp mixed spice
cream, to serve

Put the blackberries in a greased ovenproof dish and spoon over the golden syrup. Cream together the butter and sugar. Beat the eggs in a little at a time, fold in the flour and mixed spice. Add just enough milk to mix to a soft dropping consistency. Spread over the top of the blackberries. Cook in the oven at gas mark 4, 180°C (350°F) for 45 minutes. Serve hot with cream.

BLACKBERRY RICE PUDDING

Everyone loves rice pudding and this is an interesting variation. It will come out mauve in colour.

6 tbsp pudding rice
300ml, ½pt (1¼ cups) whipping cream
50g, 2oz (½ cup) icing sugar
3 tbsp blackberry purée

Cook the rice in boiling water for 10 minutes. Drain and run under cold water. Whip the cream with the icing sugar. Fold the cream into the rice and the blackberry purée. Serve at once.

BLACKBERRY BRULÉE

225g, 8oz blackberries
50g, 2oz (½ cup) light brown sugar
150ml, ¼pt (⅔ cup) whipped cream
75g, 3oz (½ cup) demerara sugar

Cook the blackberries gently with the brown sugar for 5 minutes. Divide between 6 ramekin dishes and allow to cool. Cover each dish with whipped cream and spread a layer of demerara sugar to cover the cream. Grill until the sugar is bubbling. You can either serve the brulées hot or allow to cool and chill for several hours by which time the demerara sugar will have formed a crust.

PEACHES WITH BLACKBERRY SYRUP

150g, 6oz (1 cup) sugar
300ml, ½pt (1¼ cups) water
4 peaches, blanched, peeled, halved and de-stoned
225g, 8oz blackberries
2 tbsp brandy

First make a sugar syrup by dissolving the sugar in the water over a low heat and boiling for 3 minutes. Add the peach halves and poach for 5 minutes. Transfer the peach halves to a serving bowl. Reserve 60ml, 2 fl oz of the syrup and add the blackberries and brandy. Return to the heat and cook, stirring for 5 minutes. Sieve the blackberries and spoon the purée over the peaches. Chill before serving.

PROFITEROLES WITH BLACKBERRY SAUCE

Choux pastry

100g, 4oz (½ cup) butter
300ml, ½pt (1¼ cups) water
125g, 5oz (1¼ cups) flour
4 eggs

300ml, ½pt (1¼ cups) double cream, whipped

Blackberry sauce

225g, 8oz blackberries
50g, 2oz (⅓ cup) granulated sugar
1 tbsp cornflour mixed with a little water

To make the profiteroles place the butter in a saucepan with the water. Bring to the boil and then remove from the heat. Sift the flour and tip into the saucepan. Stir until the paste is smooth. Allow to cool for 5 minutes. Transfer to a bowl and gradually beat in the eggs using an electric whisk. Beat until the mixture is smooth and glossy. Pipe or put spoonfuls onto a dampened baking sheet and bake in the oven for 10 minutes at gas mark 6, 200°C (400°F) and then for another 10 minutes at gas mark 7, 220°C (450°F). Remove from the oven and place on a wire rack. Make a hole in the side of each profiterole to allow any steam to escape. When they are cool slit each one at the side and fill with a little whipped cream. Pile the profiteroles up in a pyramid. Now make the sauce. Cook the blackberries with the sugar until the juices begin to run. Sieve the fruit and return to the pan. Heat gently and add the cornflour paste. Stir constantly as the sauce thickens. Pour over the profiteroles and serve at once.

BLACKBERRY SOUFFLÉ

450g, 1lb blackberries
100g, 4oz (1 cup) brown sugar
100g, 4oz (⅔ cup) caster sugar
4 eggs, separated
150ml, ¼pt (⅔ cup) soured cream
75g, 3oz (¾ cup) brown breadcrumbs

Cook the blackberries, with no extra liquid added, with the brown sugar very gently until the juices run clear. When tender sieve them to make a purée. Whisk together the egg yolks and caster sugar until thick. Stir in the soured cream, the blackberry purée and the breadcrumbs. Whisk the egg whites until stiff and fold into the breadcrumb mixture. Bake in the oven at gas mark 6, 200°C (400°F) for 25 minutes.

BLACKBERRY CHEESECAKE

150g, 6oz digestive biscuits, crushed
1 tbsp demerara sugar
75g, 3oz (⅓ cup) butter
450g, 1lb blackberries
4 tbsp water
100g, 4oz (⅔ cup) caster sugar
25g, 1oz gelatine
2 eggs, separated
350g, 12oz cottage cheese, sieved
150ml, ¼pt (⅔ cup) double cream, whipped

Mix the crushed biscuits with the sugar and butter and cook gently until the sugar is dissolved and butter melted. Spread over the base of a 20cm (8in) greased loose-bottomed cake tin. Cook the blackberries with two tablespoons of the water and 50g, 2oz *(⅓ cup)* of the sugar until soft. Drain off the juice and reserve. Rub the fruit through a sieve. Soften the gelatine in the remaining two tablespoons of water. Beat the egg yolks and remaining sugar until thick. Fold in the cottage cheese and the blackberry purée. Add the blackberry juice to the gelatine and place over a pan of hot water to dissolve. Strain onto the cheese mixture and mix well. Chill until almost set. Whisk the egg whites and fold in to the cheesecake mixture along with the whipped cream. Pour over the biscuit base. Chill and serve.

BLACKBERRY LAYER PUDDING

225g, 8oz (1 cup) butter
225g, 8oz digestive biscuits, crushed
50g, 2oz (½ cup) icing sugar
300ml, ½pt (1¼ cups) blackberry purée (thickened with cornflour)
300ml, ½pt (1¼ cups) double cream

Melt 100g, 4oz (½ cup) of the butter and add the biscuit crumbs. Spoon into a greased cake tin. Cream together the remaining butter and sugar until light. Spread over the biscuit crumbs. Spoon the thickened blackberry purée over the butter and sugar and then top with cream. Sprinkle the rest of the biscuit crumbs on top and chill.

PURPLE FLAN

150g, 6oz digestive biscuits, crushed
50g, 2oz (⅓ cup) butter
small tin of condensed milk
300ml, ½pt (1¼ cups) double cream
juice of 1 lemon
2 tbsp blackberry purée

Melt the butter in a saucepan and mix in the crushed biscuits. Line a greased 20cm (8in) flan dish with the biscuit mixture. Pour the condensed milk into a bowl. Whip the cream and mix into the condensed milk. Add the lemon juice and blackberry purée and blend everything together. Pour over the biscuit base and chill.

BLACKBERRY CHANTILLY

225g, 8oz blackberries
4 egg yolks
50g, 2oz (⅓ cup) caster sugar
300ml, ½pt (1¼ cups) whipping cream
50g, 2oz (½ cup) icing sugar

Rub the blackberries through a sieve to make a purée. Put the egg yolks and sugar in a bowl and whisk until thick. Whip the cream with the icing sugar. Fold the blackberry purée and whipped cream into the egg and sugar mixture, pour into a serving bowl and chill until ready to serve.

BLACKBERRY SYLLABUB

650g, 1½lb blackberries
100g, 4oz (⅔ cup) caster sugar
300ml, ½pt (1¼ cups) double cream
90ml, 3fl oz (⅓ cup) white wine

Cook the blackberries without any extra liquid in a saucepan with a tight fitting lid until the juices start to run. Sieve the blackberries and allow to cool. Whip the cream and white wine together. Fold the purée into the cream. Divide the mixture between 4 glasses.

BLACKBERRY AND ELDERFLOWER FOOL

225g, 8oz blackberries
90ml, 3fl oz (⅓ cup) elderflower cordial
150ml, ¼pt (⅔ cup) double cream
2 egg whites

Cook the blackberries in the elderflower cordial in a covered saucepan for about 15 minutes, or until the berries are tender. Remove the lid and boil rapidly to reduce the liquid a little. Allow the fruit to cool. Whip the double cream until thick and gently fold into the fruit mixture. Lastly whisk the egg whites until thick and fold them into the fruit as well.

BLACKBERRY SNOW

450g, 1lb blackberries
2 egg whites
50g, 2oz (⅓ cup) caster sugar
300ml, ½pt (1¼ cups) double cream

Rub the blackberries through a sieve to make a purée. Pour the purée into a container and freeze for 2 hours. Whisk the egg whites until stiff and gradually add the sugar while continuing to whisk. Take the blackberry purée from the freezer and mash to break down any large ice crystals. Fold the cream and egg white mixture together and fold into the semi-frozen blackberry purée forming a swirled effect. Spoon into glasses or into a serving bowl and serve immediately.

BLACKBERRY AND CRÈME FRAÎCHE MOUSSE

450g, 1lb blackberries
juice of 1 lemon
3 eggs, separated
25g, 1oz gelatine or vege-gel
150g, 6oz (1cup) caster sugar
300ml, ½pt (1¼ cups) crème fraîche

Cook the blackberries in the lemon juice in a saucepan with a tightly fitting lid. When the blackberries have softened, remove from the heat, sieve them and allow to cool. Put 3 tablespoons of water in a small saucepan and sprinkle the gelatine in. Leave to soften a little and then heat very gently until the gelatine has dissolved. Leave to cool. Whisk the egg yolks and gradually add the caster sugar, whisking until they form a thick and pale mixture. Stir in the cooled blackberry mixture and the gelatine. Add the crème fraîche and lastly whisk the egg whites until stiff and fold them in too. Pour the mousse into a serving bowl and leave to set.

BLACKBERRY ICE CREAM

An easy ice cream to make since you don't need an ice cream maker and you don't need to beat the half frozen mixture.

450g, 1lb blackberries, puréed and sieved
75g, 3oz (¾ cups) icing sugar
squeeze of lemon juice
75g, 3oz (½ cup) sugar
120ml, 4 fl oz (½ cup) water
3 egg yolks
300ml, ½pt (1¼ cups) whipped cream

Put the blackberry purée in a bowl with the icing sugar and squeeze of lemon juice. Dissolve the sugar with the water in a heavy-based saucepan and boil for 5 minutes. Whisk the egg yolks until thick and then whisk in the boiling syrup. Continue to whisk until the mixture is cold and very light and thick. Fold in the blackberry purée and cream. Spoon into a freezer container and freeze until firm.

BLACKBERRY AND MASCARPONE ICED MOUSSE

450, 1lb blackberries, puréed and sieved
3 eggs, separated
100g, 4oz (⅔ cup) caster sugar
225g, 8oz (2 cups) mascarpone

Beat the egg yolks with the caster sugar until thick and creamy. Fold in the blackberry purée. Then mix in the mascarpone and lastly whip the egg whites until stiff and fold them in as well. Serve chilled.

BRAMBLE AND BRANDY DRINK

1 litre, 1.8pt (3⅓ cups) strained blackberry juice
225g, 8oz (1⅓ cups) sugar
300ml, ½pt (1¼ cups) brandy

Pour the blackberry juice into a large saucepan and add the sugar. Stir with a wooden spoon and cook over low heat until the sugar has dissolved. Bring to the boil. Boil for 5 minutes, stirring occasionally. Skim off any scum that rises to the surface. Allow to cool for 10 minutes and then stir in the brandy. Serve hot or cold.

BLACKBERRY KETCHUP

This goes well with cold meats.

1.3kg, 3lb blackberries
water
granulated sugar
½ tsp dry mustard
2 tsp ground ginger
pinch of ground cloves
600ml, 1pt (2½ cups) vinegar

Put the blackberries in a saucepan, with enough water to come halfway up, and cook until soft. Sieve them and measure the purée. For every 600ml, 1pt (2½ cups) you will need 100g, 4oz (⅔ cup) of sugar. Pour the blackberry purée into a large saucepan, add the sugar, mustard powder, ground ginger, dry cloves and vinegar. Simmer gently to dissolve the sugar for about 30 minutes by which time the mixture should be thick. Pour into bottles and seal tightly.

PLUMS AND DAMSONS

STARTERS

PLUM MULLIGATAWNY

25g, 1oz (2 tbsp) margarine
1 small onion, peeled and sliced
1 tsp medium curry powder
25g, 1oz (¼ cup) flour
600ml, 1pt (2½ cups) vegetable stock
450g, 1lb plums, de-stoned
25g, 1oz (¼ cup) sultanas
50g, 2oz (⅓ cup) sugar
1 clove of garlic, peeled and crushed
¼ tsp cayenne pepper
salt and pepper
50g, 2oz (¼ cup) basmati rice

Melt the margarine in a casserole and brown the onion. Stir in the curry powder and flour. Blend in the stock and stir to make a smooth sauce. Add the plums, sultanas, sugar, garlic and cayenne pepper. Simmer for 45 minutes. Season with salt and pepper and add the rice. Cook for a further 15 minutes and serve hot.

ICED PLUM SOUP

450g, 1lb red plums, halved and de-stoned
2 tbsp water
75g, 3oz (½ cup) sugar
1 stick of cinnamon
90ml, 3 fl oz (⅓ cup) red wine
3 tsp cornflour
grated rind and juice of 1 lemon
150ml, ¼pt (⅔ cup) soured cream

Put the plums, water, sugar and cinnamon stick in a saucepan and bring to the boil. Reduce the heat and simmer for 10 minutes. Mix the red wine and cornflour together until blended. Pour into the plum mixture and cook, stirring all the time until the mixture thickens. Blend or process the soup with the lemon rind and juice. Stir in the soured cream, reserving a little. Chill the soup. Add a teaspoon of soured cream to each bowl just before serving.

PLUM AND BULGHUR WHEAT SALAD

75g, 3oz bulghur wheat
a handful of chopped parsley
1 tsp chopped fresh mint
juice of 2 lemons
2 tbsp olive oil
salt and pepper
4 spring onions, chopped
225g, 8oz plums, halved and de-stoned

Cover the bulghur wheat with water and leave for 15 minutes. Put the parsley, mint, lemon juice, olive oil and seasoning in a bowl. Add the chopped spring onions. Toss the plums into the dressing. Drain the water from the bulghur wheat and add to the plums. Mix everything together and serve.

MAIN DISHES

LAMB AND PLUMS IN A POT

Serves 4 - 6

1 medium sized leg of lamb
15g, ½oz (1 tbsp) butter
300ml, ½pt (1¼ cups) red wine
450g, 1lb red plums
1 clove of garlic, peeled and crushed
1 onion, peeled and chopped
¼ tsp cinnamon
¼ tsp nutmeg
1 tbsp sugar

Brown the joint in the butter. Put into a deep pot and pour the red wine over the joint. Cover and cook on the hob for half an hour. Add the plums, the garlic and the chopped onion. Cook for another hour. Remove the joint from the pot. Skim off any fat from the cooking juices and sieve the juices to remove the plum stones and skins. Season with the cinnamon and nutmeg and add the sugar. Pour some sauce over the lamb and serve the remaining sauce in a jug.

PORK IN PLUM SAUCE

Serves 4

450g, 1lb plums, halved and de-stoned
300ml, ½pt (1¼ cups) rosé wine
salt and pepper
25g, 1oz (¼ cup) plain wholemeal flour
650g, 1½lb pork fillet, trimmed and cubed
25g, 1oz (2 tbsp) butter
1 onion, skinned and chopped
150g, 6oz white cabbage, shredded
2 tbsp natural yoghurt

Simmer the plums in the wine for 5 minutes until tender. Strain, reserving the juice. Purée half the plums. Coat the cubed pork with flour and season with salt and pepper. Melt the butter in a casserole and fry the onion and cabbage for a few minutes. Add the meat and fry until brown on all sides. Pour in the reserved plum juice and puréed plums and simmer uncovered for 20 minutes. Just before serving add the reserved plums and yoghurt and reheat a little.

PORK RASHERS WITH PLUMS

Serves 4

450g, 1lb red plums, halved and de-stoned
2 tbsp brown sugar
2 tbsp sunflower oil
8 pork rashers
1 onion, peeled and sliced
2 cloves of garlic, peeled and crushed
1 tsp chopped sage
3 tbsp chicken stock
3 tbsp dry cider
salt and pepper

Place the plums in a casserole and sprinkle with the brown sugar. Heat the oil in a frying pan and brown the pork on both sides. Remove the pork and add the onion. Cook gently until softened and then stir in the garlic and sage. Add to the casserole and pour in the stock and cider. Arrange the pork on top and season with salt and pepper. Cover and cook in the oven at gas mark 4, 180°C (350°F) for 1½ hours. Baste the pork every so often with the plum juice.

BACON CHOPS WITH PLUM SAUCE

A quick, easy supper dish. Serve with mashed potato and
green vegetables.

Serves 2

2 bacon chops
75g, 3oz plum jam
2 tbsp red wine vinegar
2 tbsp water
1 tsp mustard powder
sprinkling of mixed herbs
salt and pepper

First make diagonal cuts in the bacon chops. Cook under a
moderate grill for 5 minutes on each side. Put the jam,
vinegar, water, mustard powder, herbs and seasoning in a
small saucepan and heat gently stirring all the time. Bring
to the boil and simmer for a couple of minutes. Pour over
the bacon chops and serve.

DUCK WITH PLUMS

Serves 3 - 4

1 oven ready duck
1 onion, peeled and quartered
bay leaf
cinnamon stick
4 cloves
salt and pepper
3 tbsp flour
300ml, ½pt (1¼ cups) chicken stock
450g, 1lb plums, halved and de-stoned
150ml, ¼pt (⅔ cup) port

Put the onion, bay leaf and spices in the body cavity of the duck. Rub the outside of the duck with salt and prick the skin. Roast the duck in the oven at gas mark 6, 200°C (400°F) for 1½ hours. Transfer the duck to a serving plate. Drain off the fat from the tin and stir the flour into the remaining juices. Pour in the stock and bring to the boil, stirring all the time. Add the port and plums and cook for a few minutes. Add the pepper. Serve this sauce with the duck.

PIGEON AND PLUM CASSEROLE

Serves 4

25g, 1oz (2 tbsp) butter
1 tbsp sunflower oil
4 young pigeons
2 tbsp plain wholemeal flour
1 onion, peeled and chopped
pinch of ground cloves
1 tbsp mixed herbs
90ml, 3fl oz (⅓ cup) port
450g, 1lb purple plums, halved and de-stoned
salt and pepper

Heat the butter and oil in a frying pan. Sprinkle the flour over the pigeons and fry them in the pan until brown on all sides. Transfer to a casserole. Cook the chopped onion in the frying pan until soft. Spoon over the pigeons. Sprinkle over the cloves and herbs. Stir the port into the remaining juices in the frying pan and bring to the boil. Pour over the pigeons. Arrange the plums over the top. Cover and bake at gas mark 3, 160°C (325°F) for 1½ hours. Transfer the pigeons and plums to a serving dish. Boil the juices to thicken and reduce the liquid. Pour over the pigeons and serve hot.

TURKEY BREASTS PAN FRIED
WITH DAMSONS

Serves 3 -4

Damsons must not be eaten raw but they give this turkey
dish an excellent flavour.

3 turkey breasts, cut into slices
60ml, 2fl oz (¼ cup) apple juice
3 tbsp soya sauce
3 tbsp dry sherry
1 clove of garlic, skinned and crushed
½ tsp dried thyme
15g, ½oz (1 tbsp) butter
1 tbsp oil
225g, 8oz damsons, halved and de-stoned
pepper

Put the turkey slices in a dish and cover with apple juice,
soya sauce, sherry, garlic and thyme. Marinate overnight
or for at least 3 hours. Heat the butter and oil in a frying
pan and fry the turkey until brown on all sides. Add the
damsons, reserved marinade and some pepper. Cover and
simmer for 20 minutes.

PUDDINGS

PLUM AND RHUBARB CRUMBLE

900g, 2lb plums, halved and de-stoned
900g, 2lb rhubarb, washed and chopped
300ml, ½pt (1¼ cups) water
4 tbsp sugar
1 tsp cornflour mixed with a little water

Crumble topping

75g, 3oz (¾ cup) wholemeal flour
50g, 2oz (1 cup) oats
75g, 3oz (¾ cup) soft brown sugar
50g, 2oz (¼ cup) butter

Stew the plums and rhubarb in the water and the sugar. Drain off most of the juice and reserve. Put the fruit in a pie dish. Rub the butter into the flour and oats and mix in the sugar. Spread the crumble over the fruit and bake in the oven at gas mark 4, 180°C (350°F) for 30 minutes. Mix the reserved fruit juice with the cornflour paste and heat gently to thicken the sauce. Serve this sauce, and a dollop of cream if liked, with the crumble.

PLUM AND NECTARINE CRUMBLE

350g, 12oz nectarines, quartered and de-stoned
350g, 12oz plums, halved and de-stoned
150g, 6oz (3 cups) oats
75g, 3oz (⅓ cup) butter
1 tsp ginger
3 tbsp golden syrup

Arrange the nectarines and plums in an ovenproof dish.
Melt the butter in a saucepan and mix in the golden syrup,
ginger and oats. Spread this mixture over the nectarines
and plums and push some of it in between the fruit. Bake
in the oven at gas mark 4, 180°C (350°F) for 30 minutes.
Serve hot with cream.

PLUM CHARLOTTE

25g, 1oz (2 tbsp) butter
50g, 2oz (½ cup) brown sugar
about 10 slices of white or brown bread
450g, 1lb plums, halved and de-stoned

Use a little of the butter to grease the pie dish and sprinkle
all over with sugar. Butter the slices of bread and then use
to line the dish. Place a layer of plums over the bread.
Sprinkle with sugar. Lay bread on top and repeat the layers.
Finish with slices of bread. Cover with greaseproof paper
and bake in the oven at gas mark 3, 160°C (325°F) for 30
minutes.

SPICED PLUM TART

shortcrust pastry made with 150g, 6oz (1½ cups) plain flour and 75g, 3oz (⅓ cup) margarine

450g, 1lb cooking plums
225g, 8oz (1⅓ cup) caster sugar
25g, 1oz (2 tbsp) butter
1 tsp ginger
½ tsp cinnamon
juice of ½ lemon
150ml, ¼pt (⅔ cup) cream

Halve the plums and remove the stones. Roll out the pastry and line a greased 23cm (9in) flan tin. Arrange the plums in the case. Combine 150g, 6oz (1 cup) of the sugar, the ginger and the cinnamon and sprinkle the mixture over the plums. Pour over the lemon juice. Dot with small pieces of butter and bake in the oven at gas mark 4, 180°C (350°F) for 35 minutes. Leave to cool. Whip the cream with the rest of the sugar and spread over the tart.

PLUM AND CREAM TART

shortcrust pastry made with 150g, 6oz (1½ cups) plain
flour and 75g, 3oz (⅓ cup) margarine

450g, 1lb plums, quartered and de-stoned
1 tsp cinnamon
300ml, ½pt (1¼ cups) double cream
1 egg
3 egg yolks
juice of 1 lemon
100g, 4oz (⅔ cup) caster sugar

Topping

2 tbsp golden granulated sugar
1 tsp cinnamon

Roll out the pastry and use to line a greased 20cm (8in) flan dish. Bake blind at gas mark 4, 180°C (350°F) for 15 minutes. Lay the plums over the pastry. Sprinkle with cinnamon. Whisk together the cream, whole egg, egg yolks, lemon juice and caster sugar. Pour over the plums and bake in the oven at gas mark 4, 180°C (350°F) for 30 minutes. Remove from the oven. Mix together the sugar and cinnamon for the topping and sprinkle over the tart. Return to the oven for another 10 minutes.

PLUM PIZZETTA

4 pieces of sliced white or brown bread
butter for spreading
6 plums, halved and de-stoned
sugar

Butter the slices of bread and place them on a greased baking sheet. On each slice put 3 plum halves and press them down on the bread. Fill the spaces with a sprinkling of sugar. Bake in the oven at gas mark 5, 190°C (375°F) for 40 minutes and serve hot.

PLUM AND STRAWBERRY PIE

The plums and strawberries make an unusual
combination in this recipe.

Shortcrust pastry made with 350g, 12oz (3 cups) flour
and 175g, 6oz (¾ cup) margarine

450g, 1lb plums, halved and de-stoned
225g, 8oz strawberries
75g, 3oz (½ cup) caster sugar
1 egg white, whisked
sprinkling of caster sugar

Roll out two thirds of the pastry and line a greased 23cm (9in) flan dish. Mix the plums and strawberries with the sugar and spread over the pastry. Roll out the remaining pastry and cover the strawberries and plums pressing the edges down well. Brush with lightly beaten egg white and sprinkle with caster sugar.

PLUM CRUNCH

This pudding has a layer of plums, followed by a layer of custard and a crumble topping so will fill a hungry family.

450g, 1lb red plums, halved and de-stoned
25g, 1oz (¼ cup) brown sugar
2 tbsp water
½ tsp cinnamon
1 egg
2 tbsp cornflour
1 tbsp golden syrup
300ml, ½pt (1¼ cups) milk

Topping

40g, 1½oz (3 tbsp) butter
75g, 3oz (1½ cups) oats
50g, 2oz (½ cup) brown sugar
cream, to serve

Gently cook the plums in the sugar and water until tender. Place in an ovenproof dish and sprinkle with cinnamon. Beat together the egg, cornflour and syrup. Stir in the milk and place in a pan over a low heat, whisking until thickened. Pour over the plums. Melt the butter in a pan, stir in the oats and sugar. Sprinkle over the custard. Bake in the oven at gas mark 4, 180°C (350°F) for 30 minutes. Serve hot with cream.

PLUM CLAFOUTIS

3 tbsp flour
3 eggs, beaten
150g, 6 oz (1 cup) caster sugar
450ml, ¾pt (1½ cups) milk
50g, 2oz (¼ cup) butter
650g, 1½lb plums, halved and de-stoned
cream, to serve

Sift the flour into a bowl and mix in the eggs. Add 3 tablespoons of the sugar. Heat the milk a little and gradually stir into the egg mixture. Butter a shallow dish, spread the halved plums over the base. Pour in the batter and dot with the butter. Bake in the oven at gas mark 7, 220°C (450°F) for 30 minutes. Sprinkle with the remaining sugar and serve with cream.

PLUM TANSY OMELETTE

3 eggs
150ml, ¼pt (⅔ cup) soured cream
75g, 3oz (½ cup) caster sugar
25g, 1oz (¼ cup) white breadcrumbs
25g, 1oz (2 tbsp) butter
450g, 1lb plums, sliced thinly and de-stoned
icing sugar

Mix together the eggs, cream, caster sugar and breadcrumbs. Melt the butter in an omelette pan and pour the batter in. Fry until cooked on the underside. Lay the sliced plums on top of the omelette. Finish off by putting under the grill for a few minutes. Dust with icing sugar and serve at once.

PLUMS IN RED WINE

450g, 1lb plums, halved and de-stoned
50g, 2oz (½ cup) brown sugar
200ml, 7fl oz (¾ cup) red wine
juice and grated rind of 1 orange
cream, to serve

Dissolve the sugar in the red wine along with the orange juice and rind and boil for 10 minutes. Add the plums to the red wine syrup, cover and simmer gently until the fruit is tender. Tip into a serving dish and cool before serving. Serve with cream.

PLUM AND BRAMBLE FOOL

Plums and blackberries make a delicious combination.

900g, 2lb plums
100g, 4oz (⅔ cup) sugar
300ml, ½pt (1¼ cups) double cream, whipped
2 egg whites
100g, 4oz blackberries, sieved

Cook the plums with the sugar in a little water for 10 minutes. Discard the stones and purée the flesh. Mix with whipped cream. Whisk the egg whites until fairly stiff and fold into the plum mixture. Divide the mixture into individual dishes and swirl a little of the sieved blackberries into each dish.

PLUM SYLLABUB

450g, 1lb plums, halved and de-stoned
100g, 4oz (⅔ cup) caster sugar
150ml, ¼pt (⅔ cup) water
2 tbsp brandy
2 egg whites
300ml, ½pt (1¼ cups) double cream, whipped

Place the plums in a saucepan with the sugar and water. Heat gently and simmer until soft. Rub the plums through a sieve. When cold stir in the brandy. Whisk the egg whites until stiff and fold into the plum purée with the cream. Turn into glasses or a bowl.

PLUM MOUSSE

450g, 1lb plums
2 tbsp stem ginger, chopped
2 tbsp sugar
3 tsp gelatine or vege-gel
300ml, ½pt (1¼ cups) whipping cream
2 egg whites

Stew the plums in a little water. Discard the stones and purée the flesh. Stir in the ginger and sugar. In a small bowl sprinkle the gelatine over 150ml, ¼pt (⅔ cup) of water. Place the bowl over a pan of hot water and stir until dissolved. Stir into the warm plum purée. Allow to cool slightly. Whip the cream. Whisk the egg whites until stiff. Fold the cream and then the egg whites into the plum mixture. Turn into a serving bowl and leave to set in the fridge.

PLUM ICE CREAM

450g, 1lb plums, halved and de-stoned
2 tbsp clear honey
75g, 3oz (½ cup) demerara sugar
grated rind and juice of 1 lemon
225g, 8oz (1 cup) mascarpone
300ml, ½pt (1¼ cups) double cream
2 egg whites

Cook the plums with the honey, sugar, lemon rind and juice until they are soft. Purée the plums. Beat the mascarpone and cream together and gradually beat in the plum purée. When the mixture is cool enough, transfer to a freezer container and freeze until just becoming firm. Whisk the egg whites and fold them into the half frozen plum mixture. Return to the freezer and freeze until firm.

PLUM AND PORT PARFAIT

450g, 1lb plums
2 wine glasses port
1 tbsp granulated sugar
2 tsp cinnamon
3 eggs, separated
75g, 3oz (½ cup) caster sugar
300ml, ½pt (1¼ cups) double cream

Cook the plums in a saucepan with half the port and the granulated sugar until the plums are soft. Remove the stones and purée the plums together with the cinnamon. Allow to cool. Whisk the egg yolks and add the caster sugar, whisking until they are very pale and thick. Fold into the purée. Whip the cream with the rest of the port and fold into the plum mixture. Whisk the egg whites until stiff and fold them in. Pour into a container and freeze until firm.

DAMSON ICE CREAM

This pudding takes a bit of time to prepare but is worth the effort, especailly if you have a glut of damsons.

1kg, 2.2lb damsons
150ml, ¼pt (⅔ cup) red wine
2 tbsp lemon juice
75g, 3oz (½ cup) caster sugar
4 egg yolks
450ml, ¾pt (1½ cups) single cream

Poach the damsons in the wine and with 50g, 2oz (⅓ cup) of the sugar for 15 minutes. Strain and reserve the liquid. Remove the stones from the damsons, purée the flesh and pass through a sieve. Stir in the lemon juice. Whisk the egg yolks with the remaining sugar until thick and light. Heat the cream until just below boiling point. Pour the hot cream onto the egg yolks, whisking continuously. Heat gently, stirring all the time but do not let the custard boil. When it is thick, remove from the heat and cool slightly. Mix in the damson purée and cool completely before pouring into a freezer container and freezing until firm, beating twice at hourly intervals. Put the reserved juice into a saucepan and boil to reduce it by half. Serve this damson sauce with the ice cream.

PRESERVES

CURD CHEESE AND DAMSON SAUCE

This is a nice light sauce which goes well with ice cream or as a pancake filling.

450g, 1lb damsons, de-stoned and chopped
1 tbsp sugar
100g, 4oz curd cheese
2 tbsp brandy

Place the damsons with two tablespoons of water and the sugar in a saucepan. Cook them for 10 minutes. Pour the damsons into a food processor and and process until you have a smooth sauce. Add the cheese and brandy and process again briefly. Serve warm.

SPICED PLUMS

Makes about 4 jars

This spicy pickle is excellent with duck.

1.3kg, 3lb plums, halved and de-stoned
grated rind and juice of 1 orange
grated rind and juice of 1 lemon
1.3kg, 3lb (8 cups) granulated sugar
6 cloves
1 stick of cinnamon
3 tbsp Drambuie

Place the plums in a bowl with the sugar and orange and lemon rind. Sprinkle over the orange and lemon juice and then leave the bowl covered in a cool place overnight. Transfer the fruit to a large casserole. Add the cloves and cinnamon stick and bake in the bottom of the oven at gas mark 1, 140°C (275°F) for 4 hours. When the plums are cooked leave them to cool. Stir in the Drambuie, remove the cloves and cinnamon and store the fruit in screw-topped jars for about 3 months before serving.

PLUM CHUTNEY

Makes about 5 jars

450g, 1lb onions, peeled and chopped
900g, 2lb cooking apples, peeled, cored and chopped
600ml, 1pt (2½ cups) cider vinegar
root ginger
1 tbsp cloves
1 tbsp whole all spice
1 tbsp peppercorns
450g, 1lb (4 cups) brown sugar
1kg, 2.2lb plums, halved and de-stoned
1 tsp salt

Cook the onions in some water for 5 minutes to soften them. Drain. Cook the apples in a saucepan with half the vinegar until soft. Tie the ginger and all the other spices up in a piece of muslin. Put the spice bag with the remaining vinegar and the sugar in another saucepan and bring to the boil. Simmer for 5 minutes and leave to cool for 30 minutes. Remove the spice bag. Add this liquid, the onions, plums and salt to the apples. Simmer for 2 hours until the chutney is thick. Stir to stop it sticking to the bottom of the pan. Pot and store. Allow to mature for 4 weeks before using.

PLUM, ORANGE AND WALNUT JAM

Makes about 4 - 5 jars

1.3kg, 3lb plums, halved and de-stoned
1.3kg, 3lb (8 cups) preserving sugar
2 oranges
225g, 8oz (2 cups) walnuts, chopped

Cut the unpeeled oranges in half and chop them up in a food processor. Put the plums, chopped oranges and sugar in a preserving pan and simmer for 1½ hours. Add the walnuts and cook for another 45 minutes. Remove from the heat and pour into warm jars.

PLUM AND BLACKBERRY JAM

Makes about 4 - 5 jars

900g, 2lb Victoria plums, halved and de-stoned
350g, 12oz blackberries
1.3kg, 3lb (8 cups) preserving sugar
1 tbsp lemon juice
knob of butter

Put the plums and blackberries in a preserving pan and simmer them gently for about 20 minutes. Then add the sugar and lemon juice and stir until the sugar has dissolved. Add the butter and bring the mixture to a boil. Boil fast until setting point is reached. Remove the pan from the heat and cool a little before pouring into warm jars.

DAMSON CHEESE

Fruit cheese is very rich and should be potted in small quantities. Use small moulds so that it can be turned out and served whole on a plate.

2kg, 4.4lb damsons
granulated sugar

Wash the fruit and put in a saucepan with just enough water to cover. Bring to the boil and simmer until the fruit is soft. Rub through a sieve. Allow 450g, 1lb (2⅔ cups) of sugar for every 600ml, 1 pint (2½ cups) of fruit purée. Return to a preserving saucepan and stir over a gentle heat until the sugar has dissolved. Then boil for about 30 minutes, stirring frequently and making sure nothing sticks to the bottom of the pan. By now the cheese will have thickened. Pour into moulds or small pots and cover as for jam.

PICKLED DAMSONS

Makes about 6 jars

2kg, 4lb damsons, washed
1kg, 2.2lb (5⅔ cups) sugar
1 stick of cinnamon
3 whole cloves
2 tsp allspice
piece of fresh ginger
600ml, 1pt (2½ cups) white wine vinegar

Prick the damsons with a needle. Heat the sugar and spices with the vinegar until the sugar dissolves, then pour over the damsons. Cover and leave to stand for 2 days. Strain off the vinegar into a pan, bring to the boil then pour back over damsons. Leave for another 2 days. Strain off the vinegar into a pan and simmer until it has reduced to a thick syrup. Pack the drained fruit into jars, pour over the hot syrup and cover. Keep for one month before using.